What People Are Saying About Our Books

*"Trusting a recipe often comes down to trusting the source.
The sources for the recipes are impeccable; in fact,
they're some of the best chefs in the nation."*
BON APPETIT MAGAZINE

"Should be in the library—and kitchen—of every serious cook."
JIM WOOD—Food & Wine Editor—San Francisco Examiner

*"A well-organized and user-friendly tribute to many
of the state's finest restaurant chefs."*
SAN FRANCISCO CHRONICLE

*"An attractive guide to the best restaurants and inns,
offering recipes from their delectable repertoire of menus."*
GAIL RUDDER KENT—Country Inns Magazine

"Outstanding Cookbook"
HERITAGE NEWSPAPERS

*"I couldn't decide whether to reach for my telephone and make reservations
or reach for my apron and start cooking."*
JAMES MCNAIR—Best-selling cookbook author

"It's an answer to what to eat, where to eat—and how to do it yourself."
THE HERALD

*"I dare you to browse through these recipes
without being tempted to rush to the kitchen."*
PAT GRIFFITH—Chief, Washington Bureau, Blade Communications, Inc.

Books of the "Secrets" Series

THE GREAT VEGETARIAN COOKBOOK

THE GREAT CALIFORNIA COOKBOOK

PACIFIC NORTHWEST COOKING SECRETS

CALIFORNIA WINE COUNTRY COOKING SECRETS

SAN FRANCISCO'S COOKING SECRETS

MONTEREY'S COOKING SECRETS

NEW ENGLAND'S COOKING SECRETS

CAPE COD'S COOKING SECRETS

THE GARDENER'S COOKBOOK

COOKING SECRETS FOR HEALTHY LIVING

KATHLEEN DeVANNA FISH

COOKING SECRETS

FOR HEALTHY LIVING

Featuring America's Finest Chefs

BON
VIVANT

An Imprint of the Millennium Publishing Group

Distributed to the book trade by Summit Publishing Group

Library of Congress Cataloging-in-Publication Data

COOKING SECRETS FOR HEALTHY LIVING

First printing, 1996

Fish, Kathleen DeVanna
96-083611
ISBN 1-883214-06-8
$15.95 softcover
Includes indexes
Autobiography page

Cover photograph by Robert N. Fish
Cover design by Morris Design
Editorial direction by Fred Hernandez
Illustrations by Robin Brickman
Type by Electra Typography

Published by Bon Vivant Press
a division of The Millennium Publishing Group
PO Box 1994
Monterey, CA 93942

Printed in the United States of America

Contents

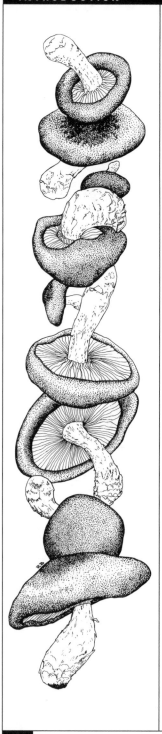

Here's to Good Food and Good Health

C*ooking Secrets for Healthy Living* is a must for every health-conscious cook. It offers an unbeatable combination—some of the finest chefs in America and their recipes for food that's healthful as well as delicious. The recipes are geared toward high flavor and low fat.

We selected 42 four-star chefs, including many of the superstars of the culinary world. We asked them for their best recipes, reminding them to be conscious of exquisite flavors in a healthful cuisine. The resulting recipes are lower in fat and calories than in most cookbooks. But the flavors are rich and enticing.

We have compiled recipes from such American cooking stars as Michel Stroot of the Golden Door Fitness Resort, Bradley Ogden of Lark Creek Inn, Paul Sartory of the Culinary Institute of America at Greystone, Charles Palmer of Aureole, Roxsand Suarez of Roxsand, Cal Stamenov of Pacific's Edge, Suzette Gresham-Tognetti of Acquerello, Alan Wong of Alan Wong's in Honolulu, and David Waltuck of Chanterelle, to name a few.

Their stellar recipes give low-fat dining a gourmet appeal. The emphasis is on fresh food, high in fiber and low in fat. To make things easy, the recipes are listed according to courses: Starters, Soups, Salads and Dressings, Pasta and Grains, Fish and Shellfish, Meats, Poultry, Main and Companion Dishes, Sauces and Condiments and Final Temptations.

You will discover a wide range of styles and specialties, drawing on culinary and ethnic traditions from around the world. And while most of the recipes stress low fat and calories, we included some fabulous desserts because we all deserve a very special treat once in a while.

Included are such delicacies as Sautéed Shrimp with Cajun Sauce and Linguine, Paella a la Valenciana, Pineapple Soup with Thai Lime Leaves and Fresh Fruit, Lemon Pepper Focaccia, Herb Spiced Venison Salad, Lobster Potstickers, Beef Tenderloins with Chanterelles and Braised Leeks, and final temptations such as a Warm Berry Sundae and Vanilla Chocolate Angel Food Cake with Bananas and Strawberries.

Cooking Secrets for Healthy Living will introduce you the seldom revealed cooking secrets from the kitchens of the finest restaurants from Maine to Hawaii. In addition, we interweave cooking advice, techniques and detailed nutritional information about each dish.

But we wanted to offer you more than just cooking times and ingredients. So we asked some of our cooking all-stars about their techniques, inspiration, advice, and how cooks at home could improve their skills. In a section we call Inside Tips, selected chefs reveal fascinating insights into how they got interested in cooking, what home cooks do wrong, what they look for in recipes, and what you can do to make your cooking more memorable.

Here's to good food and good health!

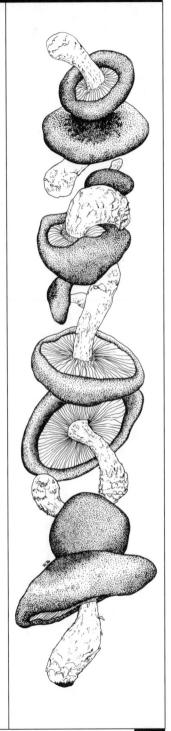

Chefs' Favorite Recipes

Starters

Eggplant Scapece—**Suzette Gresham-Tognetti**—**Acquerello**, *46*

Halibut and Spring Vegetable Ravioli with Red Pepper Coulis—**Erik Huber**—**The Fish House**, *47*

Johnnycakes with Salt Cod and Oysters—**Clark Fraiser and Mark Gaier**—**Arrows**, *48*

Lobster and Corn Fritters—**Clark Frasier and Mark Gaier**—**Arrows**, *49*

Lobster Carpaccio with Walnut Thyme Basil Pesto—**John Halligan**—
RIHGA Royal Hotel—**Halcyon**, *50*

Oyster Shooters—**Alan Wong**—**Alan Wong's**, *51*

Potstickers with Lobster in 3 Dipping Sauces—**Clark Fraiser and Mark Gaier**—**Arrows**, *52*

Roasted Oysters—**Todd English**—**Olives**, *53*

Shrimp with Prosciutto di Parma—**Michele Orsino**—**Ciao Europa**, *54*

Striped Bass Ceviche—**Fred Sabo**—**Tropica**, *55*

Tapenade—**Paul Sartory**—**Culinary Institute of America**, *56*

Tuna with Red Cabbage—**Michele Orsino**—**Ciao Europa**, *57*

Vegetable Spring Rolls—**Paul O'Connell**—**Providence**, *58*

Soups

Barley Soup with Tomato, Onion and Pancetta—**Suzette Gresham-Tognetti**—
Acquerello, *60*

Bouillabaisse—**Erik Huber**—**The Fish House** *61*

Salads and Dressings

Breads and Pizza

Fish and Shellfish

Meats

Poultry

Pasta and Grains

Main and Companion Dishes

Sauces and Condiments

Final Temptations

America's Cooking Stars

ACQUERELLO
SUZETTE GRESHAM-TOGNETTI

1722 Sacramento Street
San Francisco, California
415-567-5432

ALAN WONG'S RESTAURANT
ALAN WONG

1857 S. King Street, 5th Floor
Honolulu, Hawaii
808-949-2526

ARROWS RESTAURANT
CLARK FRAISER, MARK GAIER
& LUCIA VELASCO EVANS

Berwick Road
Ogunquit, Maine
207-361-1100

AUREOLE RESTAURANT
CHARLES PALMER

34 East 61st Street
New York, New York
212-772-0404

BELLA SARATOGA RESTAURANT
BILL COOPER

14503 Big Basin Way
Saratoga, California
408-741-5115

BISTROT LEPIC
BRUNO FORTIN

1736 Wisconsin Avenue, NW
Washington, DC
202-333-0111

BRASSERIE T
GALE GAND & RICK TRAMONTO

305 S. Happ Road
Northfield, Illinois
847-446-0444

BREW MOON
DONALD CHAPELLE

115 Stuart Street
City Place
Boston, Massachusetts
617-742-5225

CHANTERELLE
DAVID WALTUCK

2 Harrison Street
New York, New York
212-966-6960

CHINOIS EAST-WEST & SOOHOO'S
DAVID SOOHOO

1735 Arden Way, Suite 224
Sacramento, California
916-922-1660

CHRISTOPHER'S BISTRO
CHRISTOPHER GROSS

Biltmore Financial Center
2398 E. Camelback Road
Phoenix, Arizona
602-957-3214

CIAO EUROPA

MICHELE ORSINO

New York, New York
212-247-1200

COMMANDER'S PALACE

JAMIE SHANNON

1403 Washington Avenue
New Orleans, Louisiana
504-899-8231

CULINARY INSTITUTE OF AMERICA AT GREYSTONE

PAUL SARTORY

2555 Main Street
St. Helena, California
707-967-1100

DALI

MARIO LEON-IRIARTE

415 Washington Street
Somerville, Massachusetts
617-661-3254

THE DOUBLE A

MARION GILLCRIST

331 Sandoval Street
Sante Fe, New Mexico
505-982-8999

EASTSIDE OYSTER BAR & GRILL

CHARLES SAUNDERS

133 East Napa Street
Sonoma, California
707-939-1266

GOLDEN DOOR FITNESS RESORT

MICHEL STROOT

777 Deer Springs Road
San Marcos, California
619-744-6677

GRAHAM'S

KEVIN GRAHAM

200 Magazine Street
New Orleans, Louisiana
504-524-9678

GREENS

ANNIE SOMERVILLE

Fort Mason Center, Bldg. A
San Francisco, California
415-771-6222

HALCYON—RIHGA ROYAL HOTEL

JOHN HALLIGAN

151 West 54th Street
New York, New York
212-468-8888

IL MONELLO

MICHAEL CRON

1460 2nd Avenue
New York, New York
212-535-9310

LA GRENOUILLE

DANIEL ORR & MARK MATAYAS

3 East 52nd Street
New York, New York
212-752-1495

LA MANGEOIRE

RICHARD DOWD

1008 2nd Avenue
New York, New York
212-759-7086

THE LARK CREEK INN

BRADLEY OGDEN

234 Magnolia
Larkspur, California
415-924-7766

MAGNOLIA GRILL

BEN BARKER

1002 Ninth Street
Durham, North Carolina
919-286-3609

McCORMICK & SCHMICK'S THE FISH HOUSE

ERICK HUBER

206 N. Rodeo Drive
Beverly Hills, California
310-859-0434

OLIVES

TODD ENGLISH

10 City Square
Charlestown, Massachusetts
617-242-1999

PACIFIC'S EDGE

CAL STAMENOV

Highlands Inn—Highway 1
Carmel, California
408-624-3801

PITTY PAT'S PORCH
CLARENCE COHEN

25 International Blvd., NW
Rutherford, Georgia
404-525-8228

PROVIDENCE
PAUL O'CONNELL

1223 Beacon Street
Brookline, Massachusetts
617-232-0300

ROSMARINO
ROSS BROWNE

3665 Sacramento Street
San Francisco, California
415-931-7710

ROXSAND
ROXSAND SCOCOS

2594 E. Camelback Road
Phoenix, Arizona
602-381-0444

SARABETH'S
MELISSA HOMANN

423 Amsterdam Avenue
New York, New York
212-496-6280

SEASONS RESTAURANT BOSTONIAN HOTEL
PETER McCARTHY & BILLY BOUDREAU

7 North Street—Faneuil Hall Marketplace
Boston, Massachusetts
617-523-3600

TARPY'S ROADHOUSE

MICHAEL KIMMEL

2999 Monterey-Salinas Highway
Monterey, California
408-647-1444

TRATTORIA AL SOLE

VINCE MACDONALD

1606 20th Street, NW
Washington, DC
202-667-0047

TRIO BISTRO/BAR

CHRIS NEEDHAM

3990 North Swan Road, Suite 145
Tucson, Arizona
602-325-3333

TROPICA

FRED SABO

200 Park Avenue
New York, New York 10166
212-867-6767

ZARZUELA

LUCAS GASCO

2000 Hyde Street
San Francisco, California
415-346-0800

ZENITH AMERICAN GRILL

KEVIN TAYLOR

1735 Arapahoe Street
Denver, Colorado
303-820-2800

Nutrition and Health

Expert advice on diet, balance, weight management, recommended servings, exercise, good sources of nutrients and how to stay away from fats, cholesterol and sodium.

WHAT THE EXPERTS SAY

Why should you care about nutrition? According to the experts, healthful diets help people of all ages. Children who eat well grow, develop and do well in school. And adults who eat well stay healthier, feel their best and work productively.

According to guidelines from the U.S. Department of Health and Human Services and the U.S. Department of Agriculture, food choices can reduce the risk of chronic diseases—including heart disease, certain cancers, diabetes and osteoporosis—which are leading causes of death and disability among Americans.

Plus, healthful diets can reduce the major risk factors of major diseases—factors such as obesity, high blood pressure, and high blood cholesterol.

The experts say people should choose a diet in which most of the calories come from grain products, vegetables, fruits, lowfat milk products, lean meats, fish, poultry, and dry beans. One important goal: choosing fewer calories from fats and sweets.

Bodies need energy and certain other essential nutrients—and that's where food comes in. The body cannot make all the nutrients it needs to function properly, so they must be obtained from food. These nutrients include vitamins, minerals, some amino acids, and some fatty acids. In addition, food supplies such components as fiber, which is important for health.

All of these components have specific functions in the body, and they are all required to act together for the body to function properly.

Here are some things to remember: Carbohydrates, fats and proteins supply energy, which is measured in calories. Carbohydrates and proteins provide about 4 calories per gram. Fat contributes over twice as much, about 9 calories per gram. And, even though it is not a nutrient, alcohol also supplies energy, about 7 calories per gram. Keep in mind that foods that are high in fat are also high in calories. Also bear in mind that many lowfat or nonfat foods can also be high in calories.

Calorie needs vary among individuals—depending on age and level of activity. Many older people need less food, partly because they are less active than younger people. People who eat less because they are trying to lose weight must be care-

★

ful to choose more nutrient-dense foods. And, mixed with all that, we all need to be more active, because being sedentary is unhealthful.

The U.S. Department of Agriculture has developed a series of recommendations of daily servings of food for average Americans. Note that a range of servings is given for each food group. The smaller number is for people who consume about 1,600 calories a day, such as many sedentary women. The larger number is for those who consume about 2,800 calories a day, such as very active men.

The recommendations are:

❖ Choose most of your foods, (6 to 11 servings) from the grain products groups, which includes bread, cereal, rice and pasta; the vegetable group (3 to 5 servings), and the fruit group (2 to 4 servings).

❖ Eat moderate amounts of food (2 to 3 servings) from the milk group, which includes milk, yogurt and cheese; and the meat and beans group (2 to 3 servings), which includes meat, poultry, dry beans, eggs and nuts.

❖ Choose sparingly from foods that provide few nutrients and are high in fat and sugars. The size of servings varies from individual to individual, but here are what the experts recommend as a sample serving:

❖ Grain products group: 1 slice of bread, 1 oz. of ready-to-eat cereal, or half a cup of cooked cereal, rice or pasta.

❖ Vegetable group: 1 cup of raw leafy vegetables; half a cup of other vegetables, cooked or chopped raw; or ¾ cup of vegetable juice.

❖ Fruit group: 1 medium apple, banana or orange; half a cup of chopped, cooked or canned fruit; or ¼ cup of vegetable juice.

❖ Milk group: 1 cup of milk or yogurt; 1½ oz. of natural cheese; or 2 oz. of processed cheese.

❖ Meat and beans group: 2 to 3 oz. of cooked lean meat, poultry or fish. Note that half a cup of cooked dry beans or 1 egg count as 1 oz. of lean meat. Two tablespoons of peanut butter or ⅓ cup of nuts also count as 1 oz. of meat.

But what about vegetarian diets? Many people are vegetarians for reasons of culture, belief or health. Most vegetar-

☆

ians eat milk products and eggs and, as a group, these lacto-ovo-vegetarians enjoy excellent health. One can get enough protein from a vegetarian diet as long as the variety and amounts of food consumed are adequate. But meat, fish and poultry are major contributors of iron, zinc and B vitamins, so vegetarians should pay special attention to those nutrients.

Vegans eat only food of plant origin. Because animal products are the only food sources of vitamin B_{12}, vegans must supplement their diets with a source of this vitamin. In addition, vegan diets, especially those of children, require care to ensure adequate amounts of vitamin D and calcium, which most people get from milk products.

Special care should also be exercised by growing children, teenage girls and women. Many women and adolescent girls need to eat more calcium-rich foods to assure healthy bones. By selecting lowfat or fat-free milk products and other lowfat calcium sources, they can get adequate calcium while keeping the fat intake from being too high. Young children, teenage girls and women of childbearing age should also eat enough iron-rich foods, such as lean meats and whole-grain or enriched white bread, to keep the body's iron stores at adequate levels.

Here are some recommended sources of calcium. Note that some of them are also high in fat, cholesterol or both. Choose lower fat, lower cholesterol foods most often:

- ❖ Milk and dishes made with milk, such as puddings and soups made with milk. Also, yogurt and cheeses such as mozzarella, cheddar, Swiss and Parmesan.
- ❖ Canned fish with soft bones, such as sardines, anchovies and salmon.
- ❖ Dark green, leafy vegetables, such as kale, mustard greens, turnip greens and pak choy.
- ❖ Tofu, if processed with calcium sulfate (read the label).
- ❖ Tortillas made from lime-processed corn (read the label).

Bear in mind that national policy requires that specified amounts of nutrients be added to enrich some foods. For example, enriched flour and bread contain added thiamin, riboflavin, niacin and iron. Skim milk, lowfat milk and margarine are usually enriched with vitamin A. Milk is usually enriched with vitamin D.

Here are some good sources of iron. Again, choose the foods that are lower in fat, cholesterol or both:

❖ Meats such as beef, pork, lamb liver and other organ meats.

❖ Poultry such as chicken, duck, and turkey, especially dark meat; also liver.

❖ Shellfish such as clams, mussels, and oysters; also sardines, anchovies and other fish.

❖ Leafy greens of the cabbage family, such as broccoli, kale, turnip greens and collards.

❖ Legumes such as lima bans and green peas; dry beans and peas, such as pinto beans, black-eyed peas, and canned baked beans.

❖ Yeast-leavened and whole-wheat bread and rolls.

Too many Americans gain weight as they get older, increasing their risk for high blood pressure, heart disease, stroke, diabetes, some types of cancer, arthritis, breathing problems and other diseases. If you are overweight and have one of these conditions, you should try to lose weight, or at the very least, not gain any more weight. If you are uncertain about your risk of developing a problem associated with being overweight, consult a health professional.

To maintain your body weight, you must balance the amount of calories in the food and drinks you consume with the amount of calories your body uses. Physical activity is a very good way to use food energy. Most Americans today expend little energy during their work activities. Plus, many of us spend a lot of leisure time being inactive, including time watching TV time or on the home computer.

In order to counteract this dangerous trend, spend more time walking to the store or around the block. Use stairs rather than elevators or escalators now and then. Try to do 30 minutes or more of moderate physical exercise on most—preferably all—days of the week. This can include walking briskly, conditioning or general calisthenics, home cleaning, racket sports like table tennis, mowing the lawn, golf, especially if you pull a cart or carry your clubs, home repair, fishing, jogging, swimming, moderate cycling, gardening, leisurely canoeing or dancing.

But exercise and a healthful diet go hand in hand. So, while you increase your physical activity, keep a steady watch on your food intake. Here are some tips to help you maintain a diet low in fat, saturated fat and cholesterol.

FATS AND OILS

- ❖ Use fats and oils sparingly in cooking and at the table.
- ❖ Use small amounts of salad dressings and spreads such as butter, margarine and mayonnaise. Consider using lowfat or fat-free dressings for salads.
- ❖ Choose vegetable oils and soft margarine most often because they are lower in saturated fat than solid shortening and animal fats, even though their caloric content is the same.
- ❖ Check the Nutrition Facts Label to see how much fat and saturated fat are in a serving. Choose foods lower in fat and saturated fat.

GRAIN PRODUCTS, VEGETABLES AND FRUITS

- ❖ Choose lowfat sauces with pasta, rice and potatoes.
- ❖ Use as little fat as possible to cook vegetables and grain products.
- ❖ Season with herbs, spices, lemon juice, and fat-free or lowfat salad dressings.

MEAT, POULTRY, FISH, EGGS, BEANS AND NUTS

- ❖ Choose two or three servings daily of lean fish, poultry, meats or other protein-rich food, such as beans. Use meats that are labeled "lean" or "extra lean." Trim fat from meat; take skin off poultry. Note that 3 oz. of cooked lean beef or chicken without skin—a piece the size of a deck of cards—provides about 6 grams of fat. A similar piece of untrimmed meat or chicken with skin may have as much as twice the fat. Most beans and bean products are almost fat-free and are a good source of protein and fiber.
- ❖ Limit intake of high-fat processed meats such as sausages, salami, or other cold cuts; choose lower fat varieties by reading the Nutrition Facts Label.
- ❖ Limit the intake of organ meats (3 oz. of cooked chicken liver has about 540 mg of cholesterol). Use egg yolks in moderation (one yolk has about 215 mg

☆

of cholesterol). Egg whites contain no cholesterol and can be used freely.

MILK AND MILK PRODUCTS

❖ Choose skim or lowfat milk, fat-free or lowfat yogurt, and lowfat cheese.

❖ Have two or three lowfat servings daily. Add extra calcium to your diet without added fat by choosing fat-free yogurt and lowfat milk more often. One cup of skim milk has almost no fat. One cup of 1 percent milk has 2.5 grams of fat. One cup of 2 percent milk has 5 grams (1 teaspoon) of fat. One cup of whole milk has 8 grams of fat. If you do not consume foods from this group, make sure to eat other calcium-rich foods.

As for sugar, moderate use is always recommended. The same goes for alcohol, which adds calories but no nutrients.

One last topic: Salt and sodium. Sodium and sodium chloride (common salt) occur naturally in foods, usually in small amounts. But salt and other sodium-containing ingredients are often added to processed food. And many people add salt and salty sauces such as soy at the table. Most dietary salt comes from foods to which salt already has been added during processing or preparation.

In the body, sodium plays an essential role in regulating fluids and blood pressure. Many studies have shown that high sodium intake is associated with higher blood pressure, even though some questions remain because other factors may interact with sodium to affect blood pressure.

Here are some tips to reduce salt and sodium in the diet:

❖ Read the Nutritional Facts Label to determine the amount of sodium in the foods you buy. The sodium content of processed foods—such as cereals, breads, soups and salad dressings—often varies widely.

❖ Choose foods lower in sodium and ask your grocer to offer more low-sodium foods. Request less salt in your meals when eating out or traveling.

❖ If you salt foods in cooking or at the table, add small amounts. Learn to use spices and herbs, rather than salt, to enhance the flavor of food.

❖ When planning meals, remember that fresh and most plain frozen vegetables are low in sodium.

★

- ❖ When selecting canned foods, select those prepared with reduced or no sodium.
- ❖ Remember that fresh fish, poultry and meat are lower in sodium that most canned and processed products.
- ❖ Choose foods lower in sodium content. Many frozen dinners, packaged mixes, canned soups and salad dressings contain a considerable amount of sodium. Remember that condiments such as soy and many other sauces, pickles and olives are high in sodium. Catsup and mustard, when eaten in large amounts, can also contribute significant amounts of sodium to the diet. Choose lower sodium varieties.
- ❖ Select fresh fruits and vegetables as a lower sodium alternative to salted snack foods.

For more information on nutrition, consult "Nutrition and Your Health: Dietary Guidelines for Americans, Home and Garden Bulletin No. 232, a publication of the U.S. Department of Agriculture and the U.S. Department of Health and Human Services. Other sources:

- ❖ Center for Nutrition Policy and Promotion, USDA 1120 20th St. NW., Suite 200, North Lobby, Washington, DC 20036.
- ❖ Food and Nutrition Information Center, USDA, National Agricultural Library, Room 304, 10301 Baltimore Blvd., Beltsville, MD 20705-2351.
- ❖ Cancer Information Service, Officer of Cancer Communications, National Cancer Institute, Building 31, Room 10A16, 9000 Rockville Pike, Bethesda, MD 20892.
- ❖ National Heart, Lung, and Blood Institute, Information Center, PO Box 30105, Bethesda, MD 20824-0105.
- ❖ Weight-Control Information Network (WIN) of the National Institute of Diabetes and Digestive and Kidney Diseases, 1 WIN Way, Bethesda, MD 20892.
- ❖ Office of Food Labeling, Food and Drug Administration (HFS-150), 200 C St., SW, Washington, DC 20204.

When your recipe calls for:	Use
Basting fats	Oil-free marinades, stock, wine
Cheese	Farmer's cheese, low-fat cheddar or Swiss, part-skim mozzarella
Unsweetended Baking chocolate	3 Tbsps. plus 1 Tbsp. unsaturated oil or margarine for every 1 oz. of chocolate. Or substitute carob or carob powder, but reduce sugar in the recipes by one-fourth.
Eggs	1 egg white plus 2 tsps. unsaturated oil 2 egg whites for 1 whole egg in a baking recipe.
Heavy cream for cooking	Whisk 2 tsps. cornstarch into 1 cup milk
Sour cream	Low-fat or non-fat yogurt, yogurt cheese or buttermilk. Soft tofu, blended.
Ground beef	Ground turkey
Mayonnaise	Substitute low-fat yogurt
Milk, whole	Skim or low-fat milk (1 to 2%)
Pie crust	Phyllo pastry
Sauces thickened with flour or butter	Pureé vegetables into the recipe. Reduce sauce over high heat. Thicken sauces with cornstarch.
Sugar in baking	Reduce sugar in most recipes 50%. Substitute 1 cup honey for every $1\frac{1}{4}$ cups sugar.
Vegetables cooked or sautéed in butter or oil	Substitute vegetable stock.

HEALTHY LIVING STANDARDS:

Suggested Substitutions

☆

A selection of all-star chefs reveal what got them interested in cooking, what you can do to improve your skills, and specific things to avoid at home. Plus, they share some invaluable trade secrets from the kitchens of the finest restaurants in America.

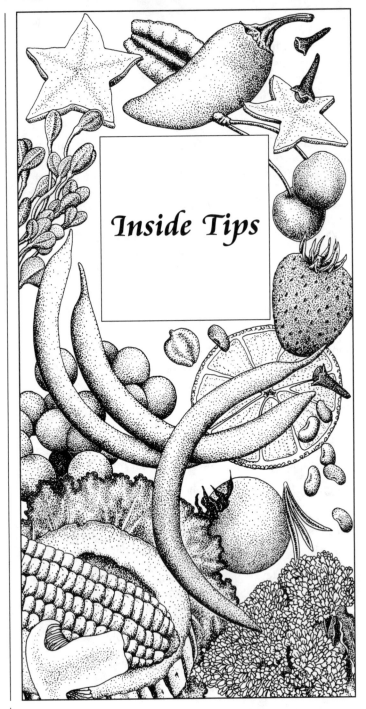

Inside Tips

BEN BARKER

Executive Chef

Magnolia Grill
Durham, North Carolina

I love the amenities of the table, the sociability, the conviviality. Growing up in a college town, restaurant jobs were readily available. The career found me. When I look at a recipe, I look for concise balance of flavors, acidity and texture—a lucid vision of how the dish will provoke response and satiation. A great cook is one who cooks with passion for the integrity of ingredients. Cooks at home should make poultry stocks, then freeze them in ice cube trays and store them in ziplock bags. Keep roasted garlic puree on hand to add savor, body and sweetness to sauces, vinaigrettes and marinades. A good quick meal: cut up cherry tomatoes straight off the vine, marinate in balsamic vinegar, good olive oil, roasted garlic, basil, salt and pepper. Then toss with hot spaghetti. Ummmmm! Three ingredients I can't live without: garlic, garlic and garlic.

★

BILLY BOUDREAU

Executive Pastry Chef

Bostonian Hotel—Seasons
Boston, Massachusetts

I do not believe in changing desserts such as cheesecakes or custards into fatless forms, as it takes away from the original premise of the dessert. Instead, I try to use bold flavors with bright and colorful presentation, as well as large servings to cancel any feeling of compromise. When I dine out, I definitely prefer comfort food, because there's still nothing better than the real thing. Cooks at home should not be afraid to change recipes to suit their own taste. I find that many of my friends who cook often miss some of the most simple aspects of cooking, that of experimenting and tasting. I think many of today's cooks are trying too hard to outdo each other in terms of how the food is presented, instead of how good it is.

★

BILL COOPER

Proprietor

Bella Saratoga
Saratoga, California

I got interested in cooking at an early age. I have always enjoyed good food and the social aspects of preparation and dining. A great cook has the ability to use spices to make flavorful foods that complement but do not overpower the basic ingredients. Good tips for cooks at home: experiment more with spices and fresh herbs, but be careful of overcooking. Make up a variety of stocks for sauces, then freeze them in ice cube trays. Afterward, keep them frozen in zip-lock bags so that you always have some handy. Many cooks go wrong because they overcook fish, vegetables and pasta. Three ingredients I can't live without: garlic, pepper and sweet basil. I rarely follow a recipe exactly, unless I'm baking.

★

CLARK FRASIER

Chef-Owner

Arrows Restaurant
Ogunquit, Maine

I became interested in cooking while living in Beijing, China. That's where I was first introduced to cooking with the season, and to the tremendous mother cuisine of Asia. Many home cooks start with a recipe, then go to the market. A good cook goes to the market first to see what is best, what is in season, then writes a menu around that. Cooks at home should learn the basics, experiment, and have fun. A good quick meal: virtually anything cooked on the grill is fast and tasty. A garlic-roasted chicken is always easy and delicious. A great cook needs dedication, speed, organization, knowledge and hard work. What makes my cooking so special? Our vast gardens, where we start writing our menus each day, plus the extensive travel we've done in both Europe and Asia, and the wonderful chefs we've trained with.

★

MARION GILLCRIST

Executive Chef

Double A
Santa Fe, New Mexico

My parents got me interested in cooking. My family always hung out in the kitchen. It always makes people feel good to eat, drink, and be with friends. I think cooks at home should always have basic ingredients around the house: kosher salt, garlic, black peppercorns, good olive oil and vinegars. A good quick meal? Pasta! If I'm hungry, I always have pasta with lots of garlic and olive oil. My cooking is special because I emphasize fresh ingredients, seasonal vegetables and fresh, local meats.

★

KEVIN GRAHAM

Chef-Owner

Graham's Restaurant
New Orleans, Louisiana

I got interested in cooking because it was a passport to travel, and then I just fell in love with it. When I dine out, my favorite type of food is Indian. I think a great cook needs imagination. A good quick meal: curried lentils and pita bread. Three ingredients I can't live without: fruit, vegetables and rice. My advice to home cooks: Don't panic.

★

SUZETTE GRESHAM-TOGNETTI

Chef-Owner

Acquerello Restaurant San Francisco, California

A great cook needs a good palate, a repertoire of culinary skills and no fear of venturing away from what the recipe says. Conceptualize instead of gluing yourself to a recipe. Follow it, learn the idea, then deviate. Many home cooks don't trust their instincts when it comes to taste. Be comfortable and confident to try what you know tastes good. People have been eating for thousands of years. It's very difficult to create something entirely new. I enjoy revitalizing and renovating old classics and personalizing them with my own interpretation.

☆

JOHN HALLIGAN

Executive Chef

RIHGA Royal Hotel New York, New York

When I look at a recipe, I look for balance, flavors, textures and presentation. Many cooks go wrong because they lose interest and become bored. Cooking has to come from the heart—that's were the flavors come from. My advice for home cooks: stay at home—don't do it professionally. Three ingredients I can't live without: fennel, cumin and garlic. In my cooking, I pay homage to the lawmakers of classic cuisine, while reflecting a belief in the cuisine of today—healthy, eclectic, imaginative, unrestricted by ethnic boundaries and always expanding.

☆

MELISSA HOMANN

Executive Chef

Sarabeth's Kitchen
New York, New York

*A*s a child, I learned to cook with my mother and father. Baking was my mother's favorite, seafood my father's, and eating mine. A great cook doesn't over-complicate a dish and mask the beauty of the ingredients. Some tips for home cooks: keep practicing, don't get discouraged, don't experiment on your guests, and increase most seasonings (salt, herbs). Many cooks don't trust their own common sense. Use your judgment, and don't always trust recipes. A good quick meal: stove-top grilled fish or chicken with steamed vegetables I think my cooking is special because I try to make the flavors have depth and clarity.

★

ERIK HUBER

Executive Chef

McCormick and
Schmick's
The Fish House
Beverly Hills, California

I'm a true believer that cooking should be fun. I love to cook at home for friends. There are so many different foods in the world, so there is always something new to try. I look for recipes that are not only user-friendly and read well, but that use ingredients I'm not familiar with. When I dine out, I love sushi. It's a great example of taking just a few fresh ingredients and combining them not only to taste good, but also to be visually appealing. Cooks at home should make sure they have all their ingredients and tools before they start. Work clean and clean up as you go. Many cooks go wrong because they either cook too hot or too cold, or they overcook the food. Three ingredients I can't live without: fennel, cumin and chives—they're very versatile and add so much to so many dishes. I think the fact that I like to cook shows through in the finished dish. I like to use fresh ingredients and combine them to get a terrific flavor.

★

MICHAEL KIMMEL

Executive Chef

Tarpy's Roadhouse
Restaurant
Monterey, California

I got interested in cooking as a child, helping my mother in the kitchen. It was something I could perform well and please others. When planning a menu, keep your guests in mind. Strive for good variety in each category. The items must fit well together. Read the entire recipe first, then go back and attempt production. Keep in mind the final product you are trying to make. A great cook has a passion for good cooking, plus knowledge of technique. Three ingredients I can't live without: fresh vegetables, fruits, herbs. My cooking is special because it is straightforward, stressing quality ingredients, freshness, heart and soul.

CHRISTIAN NEEDHAM

Executive Chef

Trio Bistro/Bar
Tucson, Arizona

My father was an Army officer, so as a result we lived in many areas of the U.S. and Europe. My mother would experiment with the local cuisines: catfish and hush puppies in Georgia, four-alarm chili in Texas, Jagerschnitzel mit spatzle in Germany, and Canard à l'Orange in France. As a little kid, I began to see the fantastic inventions that were possible through cooking. My favorite food is seafood. I could eat sushi, soft-shelled crab, oysters and ahi tuna every single day for the rest of my life. If I lived in Hawaii, I would weigh over 300 pounds. I look for easy, healthy, energy food for myself (pasta, bread, salad). I'm on the move 10 to 15 hours a day, so I can't afford to get filled up. Occasionally, on my day off, I'll indulge myself (Oysters Rockefeller). Tips for the home cook: sharpen your knives regularly and clean as you go. But, most of all, choose recipes that spark your curiosity as well as stimulate your taste buds. Many cooks go wrong by following the recipe too literally. While in the restaurant we formulate recipes so that they come out right each time, the home cook needn't be so rigid. He can add, delete, increase or decrease the ingredients as he wishes.

BRADLEY OGDEN

Owner-Chef

Lark Creek Inn
Larkspur, California

I got interested in cooking when I had a summer job as a bellhop. They needed help washing dishes, so I did that. Then they needed help making breakfast, so I helped out. After that, I fell in love with cooking and the kitchen, and I went to the Culinary Institute of America. I don't use recipes. When cooking, I try to use seasonal, indigenous ingredients, and make something simple. Cooks at home should keep things simple too— and do things they are familiar with. Many cooks tend to overdo— over-mix, over-stir and over-add. They over-play with the food. A great cook is adventurous and willing to taste and try lots of different things, in order to educate his or her palate.

☆

DANIEL JOSEPH ORR

Chef de Cuisine

Le Grenouille
Restaurant
New York, New York

W hen I look at a recipe, I look for simplicity and cleanness. If it looks like the flavors are to be modified, I stay clear. When I dine out, I prefer any thing except classical French. I love ethnic foods such as Japanese, Thai and Moroccan—and I always keep it on the light side. I believe anyone can become a good cook if he or she wants to. What makes a great cook is when the individual learns to choose the best ingredients and brings out their flavors to the fullest while retaining their simplicity and individuality. My three tips for cooks at home: cook only what you enjoy eating; cook only when you feel like cooking; and shop only when you're hungry—you become creative when surrounded by food. When having a group of guests over, don't try to do too much. Plan ahead and leave just a few final details. That way you can enjoy the evening too. Three ingredients I can't live without: hand-raked sea salt from Brittany, my seven different spice blends, and all the types of potatoes. I try to create dishes with deep concepts, without losing a sense of humor. I believe this makes my food memorable.

CHARLES PALMER

Chef-Owner

Aureole
New York, New York

A great cook should have a passion for food and taste. My tip for cooks at home: be adventurous, don't be afraid to try new recipes. Many cooks go wrong because they start with bad ingredients. Three ingredients I can't live without: onions, mushrooms and tomatoes. I am a big fan of Cervena, farm-raised venison from New Zealand. It's a very healthy meat, and not widely known. Cervena deer are entirely grass-fed to produce a tender, mild meat that requires no marinating. It cooks quickly over high heat, and should never be reheated.

★

FRED SABO

Executive Chef

Tropica Bar and Seafood House
New York, New York

I first got interested in cooking out of necessity. I worked in restaurants during high school and really enjoyed the whole atmosphere. Cooking for me was not only interesting and challenging, but when things worked out well, extremely satisfying. When I look at a recipe, I look for interesting ingredients, creativity, pure and natural ingredients that are enhanced, not hindered, by their accompaniments. Cooks at home should make cooking their hobby. Do it as therapy—be relaxed, drink and enjoy as you cook. Find some recipes you are interested in and maybe take a few basic cooking classes to learn techniques. And always start with top quality ingredients. Many cooks go wrong because they overcook food and under-season it. Three ingredients I can't live without: olive oil, sea salt, soy sauce.

★

JAMIE SHANNON

Executive Chef

**Commander's Palace
Restaurant
New Orleans, Louisiana**

I grew up on my great-grandparents' farm, and I cooked with my godmother, who was from Sicily. That's how I got interested in cooking. When I dine out, I look for authentic ethnic food. A great cook is someone who can be thrown a curve and still deliver great product. Cooks at home should adjust recipes to their own status, that is, their ovens, ingredients, etc. And be flexible—cooking is not black and white. Three ingredients I can't live without: fish, oysters and crabs. My cooking is special because we use fresh, indigenous ingredients and we keep to Creole techniques and methods.

ANNIE SOMERVILLE

Executive Chef

**Greens Restaurant
San Francisco,
California**

Cooking meals for the community Zen center and vegetarian food got me interested in cooking. When I dine out, I prefer Asian food. A great cook is one who has a great sense of taste, sensitive to what's in season, and a willingness to work with what's there. Some good tips for cooks at home: use fresh ingredients, grow or buy good produce, try a planter box with fresh herbs. A good quick meal: pasta, polenta, potatoes. What makes my cooking special is that I pay attention to all steps in a planning order. I put a tremendous amount of care into the finished product.

DAVID SOOHOO

Chef-Owner

SooHoo's
Sacramento, California

I love improvisation and customizing specific meals for customers. We Chinese don't follow recipes or do much about writing them down. We create expressions and keep those. Too many cooks use inferior equipment, and stoves and ovens that aren't what they say they are. A good quick meal: ramen with extremely expensive lunch meats. Three ingredients I can't live without: hoisin sauce, oyster sauce, and butter. I follow my philosophy of the Nine-Door theory and use it to anchor my cooking's high level of excitement.

MICHEL STROOT

Executive Chef

Golden Door Health Resort
San Marcos, California

W hat got me interested in cooking? First the prestige; next, learning techniques; third, learning cuisines of the world, and, for the last 20 years, the benefits of lighter cuisine for health and well-being. When I look at a recipe, I look for an absence of saturated fat, a balance of low fat, complex carbohydrates and proteins, with spices, herbs and seasonings. A great cook is open-minded, one who can explore and reinvent dishes, particularly seasonal foods. Cooks at home should keep it simple: have a few basics on hand, know a few recipes, and create. Many cooks go wrong because they add too much salt, overcook, or cook way in advance. A good quick meal: pasta or risotto with seafood, a salad of vine-ripened tomatoes, and lots of vegetables. When I dine out, I prefer Oriental food, mainly Thai or Indonesian, along with salads, grilled vegetables and seafood. I stay away from deep-fried food.

ROXSAND SCOCOS

Chef-Owner

Roxsand
Phoenix, Arizona

I got interested in cooking because I love seeing the bounty of fresh ingredients arranged on a work table. A great cook should have a good eye, nose and palate. Home cooks should plan their menus while at the market. Don't rush the initial cooking time of base ingredients which support the rest of the recipe. A good quick meal: pasta and stir-fried vegetables. Three ingredients I can't live without: onions, garlic and ginger. When I dine out, I look for Mexican food cooked by simple, country-type cooks.

RICK TRAMONTO AND GALE GAND

Chef-Owners

Brasserie T
Northfield, Illinois

What makes a good cook? Drive, passion, discipline, a love of eating, and good hand-eye coordination. When we dine out, we enjoy Italian beef and Jewish deli food. Cooks at home should always buy the best quality ingredients they can afford. Some cooks go wrong because they don't cook with their instincts. A good quick meal: fresh chopped tomatoes, sautéed; whisk in a little butter and black pepper. Then sauce it over linguine. What makes our cooking special is that we love to cook together. Our dishes represent down-to-earth, country cooking, based on hearty dishes from France, Italy and America. It's food that Gale and I could eat every day.

ALAN WONG

Chef-Owner

Alan Wong's Restaurant
Honolulu, Hawaii

When I look at a recipe, I look for simplicity, intrigue, availability of ingredients, level of difficulty and originality. I got interested in cooking with my first classes in ice carving and vegetable carving. Cooks at home should cook from the heart and consider the family. Many cooks try too hard. My cooking is a reflection of my upbringing, training and personality. Three ingredients I can't live without: ginger, garlic and chiles.

☆

Starters

Eggplant Scapece

Halibut and Spring Vegetable
Ravioli with Red Pepper Coulis

Johnnycakes with Salt Cod
and Oysters

Lobster and Corn Fritters

Lobster Carpaccio with
Walnut Thyme Basil Pesto

Oyster Shooters

Potstickers with Lobster
in 3 Dipping Sauces

Roasted Oysters

Shrimp with Prosciutto di Parma

Striped Bass Ceviche

Tapenade

Tuna with Red Cabbage

Vegetable Spring Rolls

Eggplant Scapece

Serves 4
Preparation Time:
  30 Minutes (note marinating time)

Per Serving:
  143 calories,
  2 g protein,
  10 g carbohydrates,
  3 g fat

  4 small Japanese eggplants or 1 large eggplant
     Oil for frying
     Salt and pepper to taste
  2 cups red wine vinegar
  1 cup granulated sugar
  1 medium red onion, peeled, sliced thin
  1 Tbsp. virgin olive oil
  10 large mint leaves, julienned

S lice eggplant, with skin, on diagonal into ¼" thick slices. Fry in oil in small batches until golden brown. Drain well on paper towels. Season with salt and pepper. Set aside.

In a sauce pot, combine the vinegar, sugar, onion and olive oil and simmer over low heat. Reserve 3 leaves of mint julienne and add the remainder to the sauce pot. Cook 20 minutes, or until onions are transparent and sauce is reduced.

In straight-sided pan, layer fried eggplant with sprinkling of mint and marinade, until it's all used. Allow to rest at least 2 hours before serving. Eggplant should be served at room temperature.

Suzette Gresham-Tognetti
Acquerello
San Francisco, California

Halibut and Spring Vegetable Raviolis with Red Pepper Coulis

I n a sauté pan heat oil over medium heat. Add the halibut, shallots, carrot, celery and onion. Cook until the fish has just turned white, about 40 seconds.

Add the basil and salt and pepper. Deglaze with white wine. Simmer for 30 seconds.

Lay out the potsticker wrappers flat and brush edges with egg wash. Place 1 Tbsp. of the mixture in the center. Fold in half to form a half circle. Press edges to seal completely. Set aside.

In a blender, purée the red peppers, garlic, rice wine vinegar, Tabasco, salt and pepper.

Drop the potstickers into a pot of boiling salted water. Cook for approximately 1½ to 2 minutes or until heated through. Drain.

To serve, ladle sauce on individual salad plates. Place the raviolis on top. Garnish with tomato and fresh basil leaves.

Serves 4
Preparation Time:
  30 Minutes

Per Serving:
  203 calories,
  16 g protein,
  16 g carbohydrates,
  6 g fat

½ **lb. halibut, cut in**
  ½-inch pieces
1 **Tbsp. extra virgin**
  olive oil
2 **tsps. shallots, minced**
1 **carrot, diced**
1 **celery stalk, diced**
½ **red onion, diced**
1 **tsp. basil, chopped**
1 **Tbsp. white wine**
8 **potsticker wrappers**
1 **egg, beaten, optional**
2 **cups chopped red**
  peppers, roasted
2 **garlic cloves**
1 **Tbsp. rice wine vinegar**
½ **tsp. Tobasco sauce, or**
  to taste
  Salt and pepper to taste
1 **tomato, chopped,**
  optional
  Basil leaves, optional

Erik Huber
McCormick & Schmick's
The Fish House
Beverly Hills, California

★

Johnnycakes with Salt Cod Brandade and Oysters

Serves 4
Preparation Time:
  30 Minutes (note soaking time)

Per Serving:
  787 calories,
  98 g protein,
  44 g carbohydrates,
  54 g fat

  1 tsp. salt
  1 cup cornmeal
1½ cups boiling water
  1 cup milk
  1 tsp. butter or corn oil
  1 lb. salt cod
  ⅔ cup olive oil, heated
  ⅓ cup heavy cream, heated
  ½ tsp. freshly ground black pepper
 12 oysters
    Red onion, minced for garnish
    Parsley for garnish

Add salt to cornmeal and pour in boiling water, allowing the meal to swell. Then stir in milk.

Heat 1 tsp. butter or corn oil in 6-inch diameter non-stick sauté pan until pan is almost smoking.

Using a 6 oz. ladle, pour the batter in the pan and sauté until the cake is a golden brown on one side, then flip. Place on sheet pan to cool.

Soak codfish in cold, fresh water for several hours. Change water and bring to a simmer in a saucepan. Simmer until the cod falls apart with a fork. Immediately drain and transfer to a mixer with a paddle attachment at medium high speed. Have cream and olive oil hot and ready. Starting with the hot olive oil, gradually drizzle in hot oil and cream, alternating until they have been incorporated into the cod. The brandade can be kept warm in a covered stainless steel pot for 30 minutes in a warm place.

Wash and crack open 3 oysters for each plate. Place them on the outside of plate out of the shell. Warm the johnnycakes on a cookie sheet in the oven. Place the johnnycake in the middle of the plate and spoon a tablespoon or two of the brandade on each cake and oysters.

Garnish with minced red onion and Italian parsley.

Clark Frasier
Mark Gaier
Arrows Restaurant
Ogunquit, Maine

Lobster and Corn Fritters

I n a mixing bowl combine the flour, salt and baking powder.

In another bowl, stir together the milk and egg. Gradually add the milk mixture to the flour, just until mixture is smooth. Stir in the lobster and corn, or yam. Pepper to taste.

In a large skillet add enough oil to cover the bottom of the pan. Ladle the batter onto the hot oil to form 4 large fritters, about 3-inches wide. Fry for 3 minutes on the first side, then about 2 minutes on the other side.

Garnish with cilantro and serve.

Serves 4
Preparation Time:
 20 Minutes

Per Serving:
 174 calories,
 16 g protein,
 21 g carbohydrates,
 2 g fat

½ **cup flour**
¼ **tsp. salt**
2 **tsps. baking powder**
½ **cup milk**
1 **egg, lightly beaten**
 Meat of 1 whole
 lobster, cooked
1 **cup corn kernels or**
 1 cup yam, raw,
 shredded
 Pepper to taste
 Oil for frying
 Fresh cilantro leaves for
 garnish

Clark Frasier
Mark Gaier
Arrows
Ogunquit, Maine

Lobster Carpaccio with a Walnut, Fresh Thyme and Basil Pesto

Serves 4
Preparation Time:
45 Minutes

Per Serving:
568 calories,
40 g protein,
9 g carbohydrates,
43 g fat

6 **lobster tails**
1 **qt. court bouillon**
3 **cups walnuts**
2 **Tbsps. extra virgin**
 olive oil
1 **cup basil, stemmed,**
 chopped
1 **cup thyme, stemmed,**
 chopped
½ **tsp. garlic, chopped**
 Salt & pepper to taste
6 **limes, zest and juice**
 Lime wedges, garnish

I n boiling court bouillon, place the lobster tails which have been skewered through the tail, to keep from curling. It is very important that the lobsters are not overcooked. Allow 5 to 6 minutes per 8 oz. tail.

Remove from court bouillon and immediately place in ice-cold water. Set aside and prepare the pesto.

In a hot sauté pan, sauté the walnuts in olive oil until it begins to smoke. Remove from the heat and let cool for a few minutes.

Grind the nuts, in a small grinder, into a paste, occasionally scraping the sides down. Place ground walnuts, basil, thyme, garlic, salt and pepper in a mixing bowl and blend with a wooden spoon to make a paste. Adjust seasonings.

Take the cold lobster tails, and with a sharp knife, slice the tail into very thin slices. Arrange the slices, overlapping them into a circle on the plate. With a small spoon, pour a small amount of lime juice over each slice, and then a small amount of olive oil. Shape the pesto into small dumplings and place around the lobster. Garnish with a lime wedge. Serve ice cold.

John Halligan
Halcyon
RIHGA Royal Hotel
New York, New York

★

Oyster Shooters

I n each of four shot glasses, place green onions at the bottom. Then add the remaining ingredients into the glasses. Be careful not to compact ingredients, so that they will exit glass while shooter is being consumed.

Garnish with chervil sprig and wasabi pearl.

Serves 4
Preparation Time:
  15 minutes

Per Serving:
  86 calories,
  5 g protein,
  5 g carbohydrates,
  4 g fat

1 green onion, sliced thinly
4 oysters
4 pieces of tomato, diced small
4 Niçoise olives
4 pieces fennel, thinly sliced
4 small pieces of basil leaf
4 pieces chervil sprig
4 pieces wasabi paste, pearl-size ball, optional

Alan Wong
Alan Wong's Restaurant
Honolulu, Hawaii

Potstickers with Lobster in Three Dipping Sauces

Serves 4
Preparation Time:
  One Hour

Per Serving:
  268 calories,
  29 g protein,
  15 g carbohydrates,
  9 g fat

1 **carrot**
4 **scallions**
¼ **head red cabbage**
¼ **head green cabbage**
4 **shiitake mushrooms**
1 **oz. package dried tree ear mushrooms**
1 **clove garlic, minced**
2 **tsps. fresh ginger, very finely chopped**
2 **Tbsps. sesame oil**
¼ **cup rice wine vinegar**
1 **tsp. salt**
1 **Tbsp. soy sauce**
1 **tsp. chile oil**
1¼ **lb. lobster, cooked and picked**
1 **package round potsticker wrappers or wonton wrappers**
   Soy sauce
   Rice wine vinegar
   Chinese chili paste

C ut the vegetables in 1-inch pieces and place in a food processor. Process until finely chopped. Place the chopped vegetables in a large bowl and add the garlic, ginger, and remaining ingredients. Check the seasonings and add more vinegar and salt if the filling tastes flat. Add the chopped lobster meat.

Place a wrapper on a flat work surface and place 1 heaping tsp. of the vegetable filling in the middle of the wrapper. Moisten the entire edge of the wrapper by dipping your finger in a cup of cool water, gently rubbing around the edge of it. Crimp from one side to the other in even folds, completely sealing the dumpling. Repeat process until you have made enough for 5 for each person or as many as desired.

Heat 1 Tbsp. vegetable oil in a sauté pan or wok until very hot. Cook potstickers for 30 seconds until light golden and then reduce heat to medium. Pour in about ¼ cup water and cover. Cook the dumplings for another minute, remove cover and serve at once.

Serve with the dipping sauces of soy sauce, rice wine vinegar and Chinese chili paste.

Clark Frasier
Mark Gaier
Arrows Restaurant
Ogunquit, Maine

☆

Roasted Oysters

Pre-heat the broiler.

In a medium bowl, combine the lemon juice, vinegar, mascarpone and sour cream until blended.

Fold in the radicchio and scallions. Season with salt and pepper.

Line a baking dish with rock salt and seaweed.

Place a heaping tablespoon of mascarpone mixture into each oyster. Set oysters snugly in the rock salt.

Broil until done, 3 to 4 minutes, 3-inch from the heat. Top with thyme before serving.

Serves 6
Preparation Time:
   30 Minutes

Per Serving:
   704 calories,
   20 g protein,
   24 g carbohydrates,
   19 g fat

24 oysters, shucked
   Juice and zest of
   1 lemon
1 Tbsp. balsamic vinegar
1 cup mascarpone cheese
2 Tbsps. low-fat sour
   cream
1 head radicchio,
   shredded
5 scallions, cut
   lengthwise
   Salt and pepper to taste
   Rock salt
   Seaweed, blanched
1 Tbsp. fresh thyme,
   roughly chopped

Todd English
Olives
Massachusetts

Shrimp with Prosciutto di Parma

Serves 4
Preparation Time:
  15 Minutes

Per Serving:
  199 calories,
  13 g protein,
  10 g carbohydrates,
  11 g fat

12 **large shrimp, shelled**
    and deveined
 6 **Prosciutto di Parma,**
    sliced in half
 3 **Tbsps. sweet butter**
¼ **cup Grand Mariner**
    Juice of 3 fresh oranges
    Ground black pepper to
    taste

rap each shrimp with the half slice of prosciutto. Sauté the wrapped shrimp in the butter until the prosciutto is slightly browned. Add the Grand Marnier and the orange juice.

Cook for about 3 minutes or until the liquid transforms into a glaze. Add the pepper to taste.

Michele Orsino
Ciao Europa
New York, New York

☆

Striped Bass Ceviche

 ombine the citrus juices and marinate fish in half of it for 30 minutes. Strain off and discard. Rinse off the fish with water.

Marinate fish again with remaining citrus juice and the remaining ingredients for 1 hour.

Serve with crusty French bread and a salad. Perfect for a summer day.

Serves 4
Preparation Time:
   20 Minutes (note
   marinating time)

Per Serving:
   447 calories,
   60 g protein,
   7 g carbohydrates,
   18 g fat

3 lbs. striped bass or any
   firm white-fleshed fish,
   diced 1-inch size.
   Juice of 4 limes
   Juice of 4 lemons
   Juice of 4 oranges
1 bunch scallions,
   chopped
½ bunch cilantro, chopped
1 tsp. crushed red pepper
½ yellow bell pepper,
   diced fine
½ red bell pepper, diced
   fine
3 Tbsps. extra virgin
   olive oil
   Salt and pepper to taste

Fred Sabo
Tropica
New York, New York

★

Tapenade

Yield: 2½ cups
Preparation Time:
  15 Minutes

Per Serving:
  126 calories,
  2 g protein,
  2 g carbohydrates,
  12 g fat

1¼ cups black olives, pitted
3½ oz. anchovy filets,
    rinsed
3½ oz. canned tuna,
    drained
3 Tbsps. capers
1 sprig thyme
1 bay leaf, crumbled
1 clove garlic, minced
4 Tbsps. olive oil

 G rind the olives, anchovy filets, tuna, capers, thyme, bay leaf and garlic together with a mortar and pestle. Slowly add the olive oil to make a paste.

Paul Sartory
The Culinary Institute of America at Greystone
St. Helena, California

☆

Tuna with Red Cabbage

Spread the cracked pepper around the loin of tuna. Saute the tuna loin on a high flame in 1 Tbsp. of the oil until just seared. The tuna must still be raw inside. Let cool in refrigerator, uncovered.

In a mixing bowl, blend the balsamic vinegar, 1 Tbsp. olive oil, salt and pepper to taste. Add the red cabbage and the beets. Mix well.

On a serving plate, make a mound of the red cabbage mixture. Cut the cooled tuna in fine slices. Spread around the mound.

Serves 4
Preparation Time:
   10 Minutes (note
   refrigeration time)

Per Serving:
   259 calories,
   40 g protein,
   3 g carbohydrates,
   8 g fat

1½ **lbs. fresh tuna loin,**
   sushi quality
2½ **Tbsps. cracked black**
   pepper
  2 **Tbsps. extra virgin olive**
   oil
  2 **Tbsps. balsamic vinegar**
1½ **cups red cabbage, sliced**
   very fine
  2 **Tbsps. beets, julienned**
   Salt and ground black
   pepper to taste

Michele Orsino
Ciao Europa
New York, New York
☆

Vegetable Spring Rolls

Serves 6
Preparation Time: 45 Min.

Per Serving:
198 calories,
4 g protein,
45 g carbohydrates

2 Tbsps. ginger, minced
1 Tbsp. garlic, minced
½ cup scallions, thinly sliced
3 small serrano chiles
2 cups diced onion
1½ cups diced celery
1½ cups shredded carrots
6 cups diced Napa cabbage
1¼ cups rice noodles (soaked)
2½ Tbsps. salt
2½ Tbsps. sugar
⅔ cup rice wine vinegar
⅓ cup soy sauce
2 Tbsps. cornstarch
3 Tbsps. water
Rice paper wrappers or vegetable wraps: romaine lettuce, grape leaves, spinach

Three Chile Dipping Sauce
6 garlic cloves
¼ cup sugar
3 chiles of choice, Anaheim, poblano, habanero, jalapeño, pasilla
Juice of 2 limes
½ cup fish sauce
1 cup water
1 tsp. rice vinegar

Heat oil in a wok and add the ginger, garlic, scallions and serrano chiles. Add the onions and let sweat for 3 minutes. Add the celery, carrots and cabbage and sauté 3 minutes. Add the drained noodles and mix in well. Stir in the salt, sugar, rice wine vinegar and soy sauce.

In a small mixing bowl combine the cornstarch with water and add to the vegetable mixture. Stir until the filling turns heavy and glossy. Remove from heat and allow mixture to cool.

Place ⅓ cup of the filling diagonally across the lower third of the wrapper. Bring the tip of the lower corner over the filling and roll once. Bring the left and right flaps together and wet each tip to seal. Roll tightly. Seal the last tip.

Sauté in oil, turning constantly, until golden brown and crisp, about 4 to 5 minutes. If you are using leaf wrappers, spray a skillet or wok with vegetable oil and stir-fry for 2 to 3 minutes.

Three Chile Dipping Sauce

Combine the garlic cloves, sugar, chiles and lime juice in a food processor. Process until smooth. Add remaining ingredients, pulse until blended.

Paul O'Connell
Providence
Brookline, Massachusetts

Soups

Barley Soup with Tomato, Onion and Pancetta

Serves 6
Preparation time:
  1¼ Hours

Per Serving:
  363 calories, 12 g protein,
  35 g carbohydrates, 19 g fat

12 oz. bag pearl barley
 2 qts water
 1 rib celery, cut into
    chunks
 1 carrot, cut into chunks
 ½ onion, cut into chunks
 2 garlic cloves, peeled
 1 bay leaf
 3 to 4 sprigs of thyme
 7 oz. pancetta, diced
 ⅓ cup extra virgin olive oil
 1 large onion, chopped
 2 cups Italian tomatoes,
    seeds squeezed out,
    juiced (reserve),
    roughly chopped
 4 cups tomato juice
    (reserved from whole
    tomatoes) strained
 2 cups chicken stock or
    water
 ½ tsp. dry red chile flakes
 ¼ tsp. white pepper,
    ground
 ½ tsp. salt, optional
 1 Tbsp. granulated sugar
 6 to 8 oz. American
    bacon, sliced, diced,
    optional
    Chopped parsley

Place barley, water, celery, carrots, onions, garlic, bay leaf and thyme in a large stock pot. Bring to a simmer. Cook for approximately 30 to 45 minutes or until most of the water is absorbed. Be careful not to scorch. Turn off heat.

In a heavy-bottom pot, sauté the pancetta in olive oil. Allow it to lightly crisp.

Add onions. Add chopped tomatoes, tomato juice and chicken stock. Allow to simmer. Discard the vegetables and then add the barley into the simmering tomato-onion-pancetta base. Stir well and keep the heat low. Season the soup with the seasonings.

To finish, sauté the bacon and strain off excess fat. Add the bacon to the soup. Adjust seasonings if necessary.

Serve with finely chopped parsley over the top.

Suzette Gresham-Tognetti
Acquerello
San Francisco, California

Bouillabaisse

Sauté the onion, pepper, celery and garlic in olive oil over medium heat until they begin to soften. Add the herbs and spices to the pan and continue cooking for another 2 minutes. Add the white wine and tomatoes and simmer for 5 minutes. Combine the stock and vegetable mixture in a large saucepan or stock pot with at least one gallon capacity. Simmer for 1 hour.

Meanwhile, prepare the seafood. Discard top shell and break whole crab sections and crawfish in broth for 2 minutes. Add remaining items and simmer. If some ingredients are cooked before the rest, remove them. However, everything should be done in about 5 minutes.

COOKING SECRET: Chicken stock, either homemade or prepared from bouillon cubes, can be substituted if you don't have fish stock.

Erik Huber
McCormick & Schmick's
The Fish House
Beverly Hills, California

Serves 4
Preparation Time:
  2 Hours

Per Serving:
  340 calories,
  44 g protein,
  11 g carbohydrates,
  10 g fat

1 small onion, diced small
½ green pepper, diced small
3 celery stalks, diced small
2 Tbsps. minced garlic
2 Tbsps. olive oil
1½ tsps. cumin
4 tsps. oregano
1½ tsps. fennel seed
1½ tsps. sage
1 bay leaf
1½ tsps. coriander
4 tsps. basil
½ tsp. cayenne
½ cup white wine
2 cups crushed tomatoes in purée
8 cups fish stock
1 whole cooked Dungeness crab
8 large prawns
16 steamer clams, about ¾ lbs.
16 mussels
1 lb. cod, rockfish or other mild fish
8 cooked crawfish

Cold Almond and Cucumber Soup

Serves 6
Preparation Time:
  20 Minutes

Per Serving:
  188 calories,
  4 g protein,
  7 g carbohydrates,
  16 g fat

¾ **cup blanched almonds**
3 **garlic cloves, peeled**
1 **tsp. salt**
4 **cups vegetable stock**
½ **cucumber, peeled,**
  seeded
3 **Tbsps. olive oil**
4 **Tbsps. sherry or wine**
  vinegar
18 **red or green seedless**
  grapes

I n a blender or food processor, blend almonds, garlic and salt with a little vegetable stock until almonds turn milky. Add the cucumber, then slowly the oil and then the vinegar. Finally, add the rest of the vegetable stock.

Serve very cold and garnish with grapes.

TRADE SECRET: This delicious and easy-to-prepare cold soup is from Andalusia, in the south of Spain.

Mario Leon-Iriarte
Dali
Somerville, Massachusetts

Fish and Shellfish Stew

In a large stock pot, heat the oil and sauté the onions until soft. Add the seafood and tomatoes. When stew has cooked through add the brandy and clam juice.

With a mortar and pestle crush the toast, hazelnuts, saffron, garlic and parsley until it becomes paste-like. Add to the stew and cook for 5 minutes.

Add the sherry wine and serve.

Serves 6
Preparation Time:
  45 Minutes

Per Serving:
  617 calories,
  55 g protein,
  26 g carbohydrates,
  30 g fat

¼ cup olive oil
1 small onion, finely chopped
½ lb. halibut, hake or monkfish, cut into 1-inch thick pieces, lightly floured
½ lb. small cleaned squid, with tentacles
½ lb. scallops
½ lb. medium shrimps, peeled, deveined
4 small lobster tails
10 scampi or jumbo prawns in the shell, deveined
10 Manila clams
5 tomatoes, peeled, finely chopped
¼ cup brandy
2 cups clam juice
3 fingers of white bread toast with a few drops of olive oil
10 hazelnuts, peeled, roasted
Few strands of saffron
1 garlic clove, minced
1 Tbsp. parsley, chopped
¼ cup of dry fino or Manzanilla sherry

Lucas Gasco
Zarzuela
San Francisco, California

★

63

Fragrant Tomato Bisque

Serves 4
Preparation Time:
  45 Minutes

Per Serving:
  95 calories,
  4 g protein,
  22 g carbohydrates,
  1 g fat

5 **large ripe beefsteak**
    tomatoes, chopped
5 **ripe plum tomatoes,**
    chopped
1 **fennel bulb**
½ **red bell pepper,**
    chopped
5 **garlic cloves, chopped**
5 **shallots, chopped**
1 **onion, chopped**
1 **qt. tomato juice**
1 **bunch fresh tarragon**
    Freshly ground white
    pepper to taste
½ **tsp. fennel seeds**
1 **branch fresh thyme**
2 **bay leaves**
1 **tsp. sea salt**
1 **to 2 tsps. tarragon**
    vinegar to taste
¼ **cup water, lightly salted**
4 **tarragon sprigs as**
    garnish

P lace the tomatoes, ½ chopped fennel bulb, bell pepper, garlic, shallots and onion in a stainless steel saucepan with the tomato juice, tarragon, white pepper, fennel seeds, thyme, bay leaves, salt and vinegar. Bring to a boil and simmer until all ingredients are very tender.

Purée in a blender and pass through a fine sieve, pressing solids with ladle to extract maximum liquid. Check seasonings, adding more tarragon, vinegar, salt or fresh ground pepper to taste. Reserve warm.

Remove the tough center core of half the fennel and slice in a fine julienne. Cook the fennel until tender in small amount of water to save maximum flavor. Reserve warm as garnish.

Heat soup bowls until hot to the touch. Ladle in soup. Spoon a bit of the garnish in the center of the bowl and top with a tarragon sprig.

Wonderful served with crunchy French bread croutons, rubbed with garlic and spread with black olive purée. May also be served cold or as a sauce for fish or pasta.

Daniel Orr
La Grenouille
New York, New York

☆

Golden Gazpacho with Tequila and Crab

Place tomatoes, peppers, cucumbers, red onions, celery and cilantro into a large bowl. Add the olive oil, Worcestershire sauce, rice wine vinegar, sugar, salt and pepper. Let marinate for about one hour.

Add the clam juice and tequila. Add all of the ingredients into a blender. Blend on a slow speed for only 2 minutes, until all of the ingredients are incorporated. Do not over purée; soup will become too foamy. Season with salt and pepper. Strain.

Serve soup ice-cold. Garnish with crab meat or any other cooked seafood.

Serves 10
Preparation Time:
  45 Minutes (note refrigeration time)

Per Serving:
  268 calories,
  10 g protein,
  11 g carbohydrates,
  18 g fat

15 Yellow beefsteak tomatoes, very ripe, diced
 8 yellow peppers, deseeded, diced
 2 cucumbers, peeled, deseeded, diced
 2 red onions, diced
10 celery stalks, diced
 1 bunch cilantro, chopped
 1 cup olive oil
 4 Tbsps. Worcestershire sauce
 ¼ cup rice wine vinegar
 ¼ cup sugar
    Salt & pepper
 1 qt. clam juice
 4 oz. tequila
 1 lb. crab meat, cooked

John Halligan
Halcyon
RIHGA Royal Hotel
New York, New York

★

Lentil Vegetable Soup

Serves 8
Preparation Time:
  45 Minutes

Per Serving:
  354 calories,
  24 g protein,
  57 g carbohydrates,
  2 g fat

3 **yellow onions, medium, diced**
3 **carrots, diced**
4 **stalks celery, diced**
3 **ears corn, cut off the cob**
1 **zucchini, diced**
1 **red bell pepper, diced**
2 **Tbsps. shallots, chopped**
1 **Tbsp. garlic, chopped**
1 **cup white wine**
3 **cups lentils, picked clean, rinsed**
1 **gal. vegetable stock**
1 **bunch thyme, cleaned, chopped**
5 **dashes Tabasco sauce**
  Salt
2 **Tbsps. black pepper, ground**
  Juice of 2 lemons
1 **bunch scallions, thinly sliced**
1 **cup grated hard cheese like Asiago, optional**

 n a large sauté pan, sauté the onions, carrots, celery, corn, zucchini, bell pepper, shallots and garlic with the wine until tender.

Add the lentils, vegetable stock, thyme, Tabasco, salt and pepper, and simmer until the lentils are soft; don't overcook. Check seasonings, adjust to suit your taste.

Serve in a heated soup bowl. Garnish with lemon juice, scallions and grated Asiago cheese.

Michael Kimmel
Tarpy's Roadhouse
Monterey, California

Mushroom Barley Soup

Soak dry porcini mushrooms in water overnight. Strain liquid and set aside. Rinse drained mushrooms and pick over to remove hard or gritty parts, chop coarsely and set aside.

Heat butter in 4 qt. or larger sauce pot. When melted, but not browned, add the carrots, onions, leeks and garlic. Cook over a medium flame to wilt and very lightly brown. Add flour and stir. Cook about 5 minutes; flour may brown lightly. Add chicken stock, whisk in the mushroom liquid and bring to a boil. Add a bay leaf, the mushrooms and the barley. Simmer for 45 minutes. Taste. Add salt and pepper to taste.

This recipe can be made with cooked beef or chicken, if you like.

Serves 4
Preparation Time:
  30 Minutes

Per Serving:
  87 calories,
  3 g protein,
  15 g carbohydrates,
  2 g fat

3 oz. dry porcini
  mushrooms
1 qt. cold water
1 Tbsp. butter
2 carrots, diced
2 onions, diced
2 leeks, washed, diced
1 tsp. garlic, chopped fine
2 Tbsps. flour
2½ qts. chicken stock
1 bay leaf
½ cup barley
  Salt & pepper to taste

David Waltuck
Chanterelle
New York, New York

☆

Pineapple Soup with Thai Lime Leaves and Fresh Fruit

Serves 8
Preparation Time:
  30 Minutes (note
  marinating time)

Per Serving:
  290 calories,
  2 g protein,
  73 g carbohydrates,
  1 g fat

10 Thai lime leaves
½ vanilla bean, split
1-inch slice of ginger
2 cups of sugar
2 cups of water
1 pineapple, sliced
1 pt. strawberries, stems
    removed, sliced thin
1 pt. raspberries
1 pt. blueberries
1 large honeydew melon,
    scooped into balls
4 plums, cored and sliced
    into wedges

 o prepare the soup base, combine in a large pot the first five ingredients. Bring the mixture to a boil. Let it stand overnight in the refrigerator.

Peel and core the pineapple. Cut into one-inch chunks. Set aside 1 cup of pineapple. Purée the rest of the pineapple until smooth. Press the pineapple purée. Then continue to add more syrup until it reaches the proper taste and consistency. Stir into the soup base.

To serve the soup, put the soup base into bowls and garnish with the fresh fruit.

David Waltuck
Chanterelle
New York, New York

☆

Pisto Manchego Vegetable Stew

In a large pot, heat the oil and sauté the onions. Add the peppers, bay leaves, eggplant and zucchini.

After a few minutes, add the tomatoes, salt and pepper, stirring well.

Over low heat, cook the stew for 15 to 20 minutes or until the liquid is almost evaporated.

This dish is delicious hot or cold.

Serves 4
Preparation Time:
   30 Minutes

Per Serving:
   329 calories,
   4 g protein,
   20 g carbohydrates,
   27 g fat

½ cup olive oil
3 medium yellow or white onions, diced small
3 large mixed bell peppers, diced small
2 bay leaves
1 eggplant, peeled, diced
3 medium zucchinis, diced small
1½ lbs. ripe tomatoes, blanched, peeled, chopped
   Salt and pepper to taste

Lucas Gasco
Zarzuela
San Francisco, California

★

Potato Soup with Gorgonzola

Serves 4
Preparation Time:
45 Minutes

Per Serving:
306 calories,
10 g protein,
15 g carbohydrates,
23 g fat

¼ **cup olive oil**
4 **garlic cloves, sliced**
1 **large onion, diced**
2 **large Idaho potatoes,**
peeled, sliced
2 **bay leaves**
1 **qt. + 1 pt. chicken stock**
Salt and ground white
pepper
¼ **lb. Gorgonzola or a**
lower fat cheese if
desired

Heat oil in a large stock pot. Add the garlic and cook until lightly browned. Add the onions, reduce heat and cook until the onions are soft and translucent. Add the potatoes, bay leaves and 1 qt. of stock to pot. Bring to a boil, reduce heat and cook until the potatoes are very soft.

Let soup cool. Purée in batches in a blender.

If consistency is too thick, use some of the reserved stock to adjust it. Season to taste with salt and white pepper.

Before serving, bring the soup back to a boil.

Ladle into bowls, crumble cheese, amount to taste, over soup. Sprinkle with chopped parsley.

Michael Cron
Il Monello
New York, New York

☆

Roasted Potato and Garlic Soup

I n a large bowl, combine the potatoes and half of the vegetable oil. Season with salt and pepper. Spread potatoes onto a baking sheet and place into the pre-heated oven. Bake until potatoes are dark brown around the edges, but not black, about 30 to 40 minutes.

While potatoes are cooking, heat a large soup pot over medium-high heat with the remaining oil in it. Add the onions and cook until they are a nutty brown color, stirring frequently. When both the potatoes and the onions are ready, combine them in the soup pot. Add the roasted garlic, chicken stock, bay leaves, thyme, salt and pepper, and reduce heat to medium. Cook over low heat for 30 minutes. Pureé and pass through a fine sieve. Adjust the seasonings if necessary.

In a large bowl, combine the diced baguette and the olive oil. Season lightly with salt and pepper. Bake in a 425° oven until they are crisp and golden brown, about 20 minutes.

Ladle soup into bowls. Top with croutons and chopped parsley.

COOKING SECRET: To roast garlic, simply wrap the garlic in aluminum foil and bake at about 350° until soft, about 1 hour.

Serves 4
Preparation time:
1¼ **Hours**
Pre-heat oven to 425°.

Per Serving:
415 calories,
14 g protein,
48 g carbohydrates,
19 g fat

4 **Idaho baking potatoes, peeled, cut into 1-inch cubes**
4 **Tbsps. vegetable oil**
  Kosher salt, to taste
  Fresh cracked black pepper, to taste
2 **onions, julienned**
3 **roasted garlic cloves (recipe follows)**
8 **cups chicken stock, (if canned, use low-salt only)**
2 **bay leaves**
1 **tsp. fresh thyme, chopped**
½ **loaf baguette, diced ¾-inch cubes**
3 **Tbsps. extra virgin olive oil**
1 **tsp. chopped parsley**

Peter McCarthy
Seasons
The Bostonian Hotel
Boston, Massachusetts

☆

Vegetable Stock

Yields: 6 cups
Preparation Time:
   45 Minutes

Per Serving:
   68 calories,
   2 g protein,
   16 g carbohydrates

3 leeks, trimmed, washed,
   sliced crosswise
2 carrots, peeled, sliced
   thin
2 ribs of celery, diced
1 onion, peeled, sliced
1 lb. ripe tomatoes, cored,
   rough-chopped
6 whole peppercorns
2 cloves garlic, mashed
½ tsp. crushed red
   pepper flakes
6 parsley sprigs
4 thyme sprigs
2 bay leaves
6 cups cold water

n a large stock pot combine all the ingredients. Bring mixture to a boil and simmer 30 minutes. Strain, cool and refrigerate, if not using immediately.

Ben Barker
Magnolia Grill
Durham, North Carolina

★

Summer Shell Bean Minestrone

I n a non-reactive heavy stock pot, heat the olive oil over medium heat. Add the bay leaf, leeks, onion, and red pepper. Cook, covered, over low heat until softened. Raise heat to medium and stir in the red pepper flakes, fennel seeds and garlic. Cook for 1 minute.

Add the lima beans, peas and vegetable stock. Bring to a boil, skim and reduce heat to a simmer. Cook 10 to 20 minutes, or until the beans are tender.

While beans are cooking, sauté the mushrooms in olive oil until crisp and cooked through. Set aside.

When beans are done, stir in the cooked mushrooms, corn, tomato, parsley and basil and simmer for 3 to 4 minutes. Season to taste with salt and fresh black pepper.

Ladle into bowls, garnish with shaved cheese. Serve with tomato bruschetta, recipe follows.

COOKING SECRET: This soup is wonderful prepared a day in advance.

Ben Barker
Magnolia Grill
Durham, North Carolina

Serves 8
Preparation Time:
   45 Minutes

Per Serving:
   188 calories,
   5 g protein,
   26 g carbohydrates,
   7 g fat

4 Tbsps. olive oil
1 bay leaf
2 leeks, trimmed, quartered, cleaned, sliced crosswise
1 onion, diced
1 red pepper, diced
¼ tsp. red pepper flakes
½ tsp. fennel seeds, crushed
2 Tbsps. garlic, minced
2 cups fresh lima beans
1 cup fresh peas or black-eyed peas
4 cups vegetable stock
½ lb. chanterelle or shiitake mushrooms, trimmed, sliced
½ cup corn kernels
1 cup chopped tomatoes
½ cup flat leaf parsley, chopped
½ cup fresh basil leaves, chopped
   Salt and black pepper to taste
   Shaved Sonoma dry jack cheese, optional
   Tomato bruschetta, recipe follows

Tomato Bruschetta

Serves 8
Preparation Time:
10 Minutes

Per Serving:
124 calories,
4 g protein,
21 g carbohydrates,
3 g fat

8 slices semolina
   baguette, grilled or
   toasted, rubbed with
   garlic and olive oil
4 ripe tomatoes, peeled,
   seeded, chopped
2 Tbsps. basil, chopped
   Salt and pepper to taste
1 Tbsp. extra virgin
   olive oil

 In a mixing bowl, combine the tomatoes, basil, salt, pepper and olive oil.

Ben Barker
Magnolia Grill
Durham, North Carolina

✩

Salads and Dressings

Ahi Tuna with Vegetable Salad and Ginger Glaze

Barbecued Pork with Watercress and Bleu Cheese

Bulgur Wheat Salad, Grilled Tuna, Sautéed Spinach, Tomato Vinaigrette

Fennel and Blood Orange Salad

Fig Slaw

Greek Brown Rice Salad

Grilled Chevre with Grape Salad

Grilled Roasted Salmon Salad

Herb Spiced Venison Salad

Jicama Salad

Papaya Carrot Salad

Roasted Red Pepper Salad

Rosemary Vinaigrette

Scallop Salad

Smoked Salmon and Roasted Lobster Salad

Sweet Potato Salad

Szechuan Cabbage Salad

Tuna Marinated in Sake with a Shiitake Salad

Fire Roasted Ahi Tuna Tenderloin with Chopped Vegetable Salad & Ginger Glaze

Serves 6
Preparation Time: 45 Min.

Per Serving:
276 calories, 29 g protein,
31 g carbohydrates, 6 g fat

- 1 lb. tuna filet, trimmed 2½-inches thick and 8-inches long
- 2 Tbsps. extra virgin olive oil
  Kosher salt
  Fresh black pepper
- 1 cup asparagus, blanched, cut into ½-inch dice
- 12 baby artichokes, cooked, cut in half
- 1 red bell pepper, roasted, diced
- ½ cup fava beans, blanched
- 1 cup Blue Lake beans, snapped, blanched
- 1 bunch golden beets, blanched
- 1 bunch Chioggia beets, blanched
- 2 fennel, peeled, chopped
- ½ bunch watercress, broken into small stems
- ½ cup tomato concassé
- 3 Tbsps. Italian parsley
- 3 Tbsps. tarragon, chopped
- 2 Tbsps. lemon juice
  Ginger Glaze, recipe follows

Brush the tuna with some olive oil and season with salt and pepper. Set aside.

Combine the remaining ingredients in a large mixing bowl and season with salt and pepper. Set aside.

Grill the tuna over very hot coals until rare. While grilling, bast the tuna with the ginger glaze.

Arrange the salad on serving plates and top with 2 slices of tuna. Finish by brushing a little glaze on the tuna and serve.

Bradley Ogden
The Lark Creek Inn
Larkspur, California

☆

Ginger Glaze

ombine all ingredients in a saucepan over medium heat and reduce to ⅓ cup of glaze. Strain.

Yield: ⅓ cup
Preparation Time:
  20 Minutes

Per Serving:
  70 calories,
  1 g protein,
  6 g carbohydrates

1 tsp. mustard seed
½ ancho chile, seeded
2 Tbsps. molasses
1 tsp. soy sauce
1 Tbsp. minced lemon grass
1 tsp. garlic, minced
3 Tbsps. white ginger, grated
1 cup sweet rice wine vinegar
4 Tbsps. lemon juice
4 Tbsps. cilantro, chopped
½ tsp. red pepper flakes
1 cup water

Bradley Ogden
The Lark Creek Inn
Larkspur, California

Warm Shredded Barbecued Pork on Watercress

Serves 6
Preparation Time:
  1½ Hours
Pre-heat oven to 350°

Per Serving:
  501 calories,
  51 g protein,
  13 g carbohydrates,
  26 g fat

  2 lbs. pork loin, boneless,
    skin removed
 12 plum tomatoes
  4 tomatillos
  4 Anaheim peppers
  1 onion
  1 carrot
    Small bunch fresh
    cilantro, roughly
    chopped
 ½ cup red wine vinegar
  2 Tbsps. tomato paste
  2 Tbsps. brown sugar
  1 tsp. chipotle pepper
    purée
    Salt & pepper to taste
  3 bunches fresh
    watercress, well
    cleaned
  1 cup Wisconsin bleu
    cheese, crumbled,
    optional
    Vinaigrette

S lice the tomatoes, tomatillo, peppers, onion and carrot lengthwise. On a pre-heated grill, grill the vegetables until they turn lightly brown.

Place the vegetables in a stockpot and add the cilantro, vinegar, tomato paste, brown sugar, chipotle pepper, salt and pepper, bringing the barbecue sauce to a boil. Using a blender, purée the entire mixture and strain well.

Spread some of the barbecue sauce over the pork loin and place in a Pre-heated oven for about 40 minutes. While the pork is in the oven, keep basting with the remaining barbecue sauce.

When the loin of pork is finished, let sit at room temperature for about 30 minutes. Slice the loin into ¼-inch slices, then julienne.

To serve, place hot shredded pork over the watercress. Top with bleu cheese and vinaigrette of choice.

John Halligan
Halcyon
RIHGA Royal Hotel
New York, New York

Bulgur Wheat Salad with Grilled Tuna & Sautéed Spinach in a Tomato Vinaigrette

L ightly rub olive oil on tuna steaks and season with salt and pepper. Refrigerate until grilling.

In a small saucepan, combine the bulgur with water. Bring to a boil over high heat and cook for 1 minute. Remove from heat, cover and set aside for 15 to 20 minutes, until the water is absorbed.

Sauté spinach in 1 Tbsp. olive oil over medium heat. Remove from heat and set aside.

Sear the tuna steaks on a hot grill or fry pan and cook to desired doneness.

To serve, place the cracked wheat salad in the middle of each plate. Place the grilled tuna on top of the cracked wheat salad and place the sautéed spinach on both sides. Drizzle the tomato vinaigrette on top of tuna and on plate.

Serves
Preparation Time:
  45 Minutes

Per Serving:
  333 calories,
  48 g protein,
  17 g carbohydrates,
  9 g fat

4 **Tuna steaks**
2 **Tbsps. olive oil**
    Salt and pepper to taste
⅓ **cup bulgur wheat**
¾ **cup water**
2 **lbs. spinach, washed**
    Tomato vinaigrette,
    recipe follows

Melissa Homann
Sarabeth's
New York, New York

★

79

Tomato Vinaigrette

Yields: 2 Cups
Preparation Time:
  10 Minutes

Per Serving:
  272 calories,
  1 g protein,
  4 g carbohydrates,
  28 g fat

4 Tbsps. lime juice
4 Tbsps. lemon juice
2 shallots, minced
1 garlic clove, minced
2 tsps. Dijon mustard
1 tsp. sugar
1 cup extra virgin olive oil
2 cups diced tomatoes
¼ cup basil, chiffonade
¼ cup mint, chopped

hisk ingredients together.

Melissa Homann
Sarabeth's
New York, New York

★

Fennel & Blood Orange Salad

R emove the skin and pith from the blood oranges in clean rounded strokes; take care not to waste any flesh. Also pay attention to not touching oranges with garlic or any other pungent flavors.

Choose firm, round heads of fennel which are heavy for their size. Trim and core each bulb and slice paper-thin.

Layer the ribbons of fennel with one sliced date and two toasted almonds. Set aside.

Prepare the vinaigrette by combining the vinegar, orange juice, olive oil and cheese.

Serve on a bed of lettuce on a large chilled plate. Dress the oranges with 2 Tbsps. of the vinaigrette. Lay down the fennel, almonds and dates and drizzle another 2 Tbsps. of dressing.

Serves 4
Preparation Time:
   20 Minutes

Per Serving:
   610 calories,
   9 g protein,
   48 g carbohydrates,
   42 g fat

1½ **lb. blood oranges, peeled, sliced rounds**
2 **fennel bulbs, chilled & thinly sliced**
4 **dates, pitted, sliced**
8 **almonds, toasted, sliced**
½ **cup balsamic vinegar**
   Juice of 3 blood oranges
1 **cup extra virgin olive oil**
¼ **cup Parmesan cheese, optional**
½ **lb. salad mix**

Ross Browne
Rosmarino
San Francisco, California

☆

81

Fig Slaw

Serves 4
Preparation Time:
  10 Minutes

Per Serving:
  37 calories,
  28 g protein,
  7 g carbohydrates

3 **fresh figs**
   Juice and zest of
   1 lemon
1 **cup cabbage, finely**
   shredded
½ **cup pumpkin seeds,**
   toasted

n a food processor, purée the figs. Combine the fig purée with the lemon juice, zest, cabbage and pumpkin seeds.

Roxsand Scocos
Roxsand
Phoenix, Arizona

☆

Greek Brown Rice Salad

Boil water, add rice and cook like pasta in plenty of water until tender but not mushy.

While rice is cooking, cut all the vegetables and de-pit the olives.

In a mixing bowl prepare the vinaigrette by mixing together the lemon juice, salt and pepper, mustard, oregano, basil, garlic and oil. Set aside

Drain rice in a colander and cool on a cookie sheet until warm.

Add all the vegetables: parsley, scallions, cheese and beans. Finish with the vinaigrette.

Serve on a bed of lettuce.

Serves 4
Preparation Time:
  1½ Hours

Per Serving:
  638 calories,
  18 g protein,
  96 g carbohydrates,
  21 g fat

  5 cups boiling water
  2 cups brown rice
  ½ lb. green beans, cooked, cut in ½-inch pieces
  1 green pepper, finely chopped
  1 red pepper, finely chopped
  1 tomato, chopped
  12 black Greek olives
  2 tsps. lemon juice
  ½ tsp. Kosher salt
  ½ tsp. black pepper
  ½ tsp. Dijon mustard
  ½ tsp. oregano, dried
  2 Tbsps. fresh basil, finely chopped
  1 clove garlic, mashed
  3 Tbsps. extra virgin olive oil
  ½ cup parsley, freshly chopped
  ½ bunch scallions, thinly sliced on the bias
  ½ cup feta cheese
  1 cup cooked garbanzo beans
      Romaine or Boston lettuce

Donald Chapelle
Brew Moon
Boston, Massachusetts

☆

Grilled Chèvre Wrapped in Wine Leaves with Grape Salad

Serves 6
Preparation Time:
  20 Minutes

Per Serving:
  416 calories,
  13 g protein,
  26 g carbohydrates,
  30 g fat

6 **large grape leaves rinse off brine in cold water)**
¾ **lb. goat cheese**
  Black pepper, freshly ground
  Marjoram, freshly chopped
½ **cup olive oil**
⅓ **cup balsamic vinegar**
½ **lb. Thompson grapes**
½ **lb. Concord grapes**
½ **lb. Red Flame grapes**
½ **lb. salad mix, mesculun**

R inse the brine off grape leaves with cold water. Cut the goat cheese to 2-ounce rounds. Season with fresh ground black pepper and fresh chopped marjoram. Wrap the goat cheese in the grape leaves and lightly coat with 2 Tbsps. olive oil and 2 Tbsps. balsamic vinegar. Set aside.

Take half of the assorted grapes off the stems and place in a food processor. Drizzle in ¼ cup balsamic vinegar and ⅓ cup olive oil and pulse. Pass the mixture through a fine mesh strainer. Set aside.

Take the remaining grapes and cut in half lengthwise. Remove any seeds. Toss together with field greens, grape purée, freshly chopped marjoram, salt and fresh ground pepper.

Arrange on serving plate.

Grill goat cheese wrapped in grape leaves over heat on a wood-burning grill. When slightly charred and warm thoroughly, place on salad and serve.

Bradley Ogden
The Lark Creek Inn
Larkspur, California

☆

Grilled Roasted Salmon Salad

Place the salmon on an oiled grill-safe pan, skin side down. Sprinkle the meat side with fennel seeds, celery seeds, thyme, salt and pepper. Refrigerate.

Bring potatoes to a boil in salted water. Turn off the burner and allow them to sit in the hot water for a few minutes until tender and done. Remove from water and set aside.

Sauté the fennel and mushrooms briefly in 1 Tbsp. olive oil, seasoning with salt and pepper. Set aside.

Rub peppers with olive oil and roast over open flame, blistering the skin. Place them in a paper bag, allowing them to steam. After 15 minutes, peel off the charred and blistered skin. Remove the top and cut into large seedless wedges. Set peppers aside.

Prepare the vinaigrette by combining the shallots, red wine vinegar, lemon zest, lemon juice and rosemary in medium-sized bowl. Whisk in the olive oil. Add salt and pepper to taste. Adjust the acidity, if desired.

Place salmon on a low-temperature outdoor grill, with wood chips smoking on the coals. Cover the grill, allowing the salmon to cook slowly and absorb smoke. Check for doneness after 5 to 10 minutes. Break filet into 6 approximately equal portions.

To serve, combine the arugula, shaved fennel, mushrooms, roast peppers and potatoes in a large bowl and toss with the rosemary vinaigrette. Place the salad on large plates with a chunk of warm salmon on top of each salad, spice-crusted side up. Drizzle vinaigrette directly on the salmon and serve.

Serves 6
Preparation Time:
 45 Minutes

Per Serving:
 716 calories,
 53 g protein,
 32 g carbohydrates,
 42 g fat

3 lbs. salmon filet,
  skin on
1 tsp. whole fennel seeds
½ tsp. celery seeds
1 Tbsp. fresh thyme or ½
  tsp. dried thyme
  Salt and fresh ground
  black pepper to taste
2 lbs. new potatoes, sliced
  into ¼-inch thick
  rounds
1 fresh fennel bulb, cored,
  thin slices lengthwise.
1 lb. wild mushrooms,
  sliced
3 red bell peppers
2 Tbsps. minced
  shallots
¼ cup red wine vinegar
  Zest of 2 lemons
2 tsps. lemon juice
1 Tbsp. rosemary, coarsely
  chopped
¾ cup olive oil
1 lb. bag mesquite or oak
  chips, soaked in water
1 lb. arugula

Ben Barker
Magnolia Grill
Durham, North Carolina
☆

Salad of Herb-Spiced Venison with Red Onion & New Potato Salad

Serves 4
Preparation Time:
  45 Minutes

Per Serving:
  263 calories,
  22 g protein,
  30 g carbohydrates,
  5 g fat

½ tsp. cracked black pepper
½ tsp. ground cumin
½ tsp. allspice
1 tsp. salt
4 medium red bliss potatoes
1 Tbsp. vegetable oil
2 small red onions, peeled, quartered
4 blocks of venison, cut from loin or leg, 3 oz. each, 1½-inch thick
20 arugula leaves
Vinaigrette (see below)

Vinaigrette
6 Tbsps. extra virgin olive oil
2 Tbsps. red wine vinegar
1 Tbsp. Worcestershire sauce
½ Tbsp. Kosher salt
½ tsp. black pepper, milled
1 Tbsp. chives, finely minced

I n a bowl combine a spice mixture of pepper, cumin and allspice. Set aside.

In a pot of salted water, bring potatoes to a boil and simmer for 15 to 18 minutes. Drain and cool.

Heat ½ Tbsp. oil in a sauté pan, and sauté the onions on all sides until browned and slightly soft, about 15 minutes. Set aside and keep warm.

Rub the spice mixture onto the venison. In the same sauté pan, heat the remaining ½ Tbsp. oil and sear the venison on all sides until brown, about 1 minute for each side. Cook to medium rare, 6 to 7 minutes total. Let the meat rest.

To serve, arrange the arugula on a plate in a circle. Slice potatoes ½-inch thick and fan over the arugula. Place 2 quartered onions in center of each plate. Slice the venison against the grain and fan slices over the onions. Spoon the vinaigrette over top.

Vinaigrette

Prepare a vinaigrette by combining all ingredients except chives. Add the chives just prior to serving.

Charles Palmer
Aureole
New York, New York

✩

Jicama Salad

I n a salad bowl, gently toss together the jicama, oranges, apple and watercress.

Prepare the vinaigrette by combining the lime juice, jalapeño, cider vinegar, sugar, salt and pepper with the olive oil. Add the remaining ingredients according to personal taste.

Serves 4
Preparation Time:
  20 Minutes

Per Serving:
  342 calories,
  2 g protein,
  25 g carbohydrates,
  27 g fat

1 **medium jicama, peeled, sliced**
2 **navel oranges or tangerines, peeled, sectioned**
1 **tart apple, cut in wedges**
1 **bunch watercress, washed, large stems removed**
  Juice of 1 lime
1 **jalapeño, minced**
1 **Tbsp. cider vinegar**
2 **Tbsps. sugar, to taste**
  Salt and pepper
½ **cup olive oil**
  Chili powder, minced garlic clove, cumin powder for more complex taste.

Melissa Homann
Sarabeth's
New York, New York
☆

Papaya Carrot Salad

Serves 4
Preparation Time:
  15 Minutes

Per Serving:
  84 calories,
  1 g protein,
  21 g carbohydrates

1 ripe papaya
1 green papaya
4 large carrots,
    shredded
    Juice of 1 lime
1 Tbsp. rice wine vinegar
1 Tbsp. sugar
1 bunch fresh cilantro,
    finely chopped

P eel both papayas and thinly slice them, removing the seeds.

Put the fruit in a bowl. Add the carrots, lime juice and vinegar. Sprinkle with sugar, then stir in chopped cilantro.

Clark Frasier
Mark Gaier
Arrows
Ogunquit, Maine

Roasted Red Pepper Salad

Place the red peppers on a grill or under a broiler until the skins are blackened. Place in a bowl and cover with plastic wrap until peppers are cool enough to handle. Remove the skins and seeds, then julienne.

In a separate bowl, mix the peppers with the remaining ingredients except the greens.

Toss with the greens and serve.

Serves 6
Preparation Time:
  20 Minutes

Per Serving:
  195 calories,
  2 g protein,
  8 g carbohydrates,
  18 g fat

6 large red bell peppers
1 large red onion, thinly
   sliced
3 scallions, finely
   chopped
3 Tbsps. lemon juice
2 Tbsps. lemon zest
2 Tbsps. lamb marinade
   (See recipe for Lamb
   Sandwich, p. 136)
½ cup olive oil
1 lb. salad greenss

Todd English
Olives
Charlestown, Massachusetts

☆

Rosemary Vinaigrette

Yield: 1 cup
Preparation Time:
  5 Minutes

¾ **cup extra virgin olive oil**
⅓ **cup balsamic vinegar or**
    sherry wine vinegar
1 **tsp. chopped rosemary**
    Salt and freshly ground
    pepper to taste

Place all the ingredients in a small bowl. Hold a wire whisk upright in the bowl, and rotate it between the palms of your hands until the vinaigrette is well blended.

Cal Stamenov
Highlands Inn, Pacific's Edge
Carmel, California

★

Scallop Salad

Bread the scallops by dipping in flour, then egg, and sautéing gently in olive oil. When golden brown, place scallops in a baking dish and finish in the oven for 1 minute.

Toss the salad mix with olive oil and balsamic vinegar to taste. Season with salt and pepper.

In a mixing bowl combine the tomatoes, garlic, herbs and lemon juice.

To serve, place salad on individual plates. Spoon the tomato mixture on salad and top with scallops.

Serves 4
Preparation Time:
   45 Minutes

Per Serving:
   431 calories,
   22 g protein,
   47 g carbohydrates,
   20 g fat

   8 large scallops
   2 eggs, beaten
      Flour
   ¾ lb. salad mix: chicory, oak leaf, arugula, etc.
   4 Tbsps. olive oil
   2 Tbsps. balsamic vinegar
   24 medium tomatoes, skinned and seeded
   1 Tbsp. garlic, crushed
   1 Tbsp. chopped tarragon
   1 Tbsp. coriander, crushed
   1 Tbsp. chopped basil
      Juice of 1 lemon

Christopher Gross
Christopher's
Phoenix, Arizona

☆

Smoked Salmon and Roasted Lobster Salad with Endive, Fresh Asparagus and Caviar Crème Fraîche

Serves 4
Preparation Time:
  35 Minutes

Per Serving:
  793 calories,
  136 g protein,
  15 g carbohydrates,
  18 g fat

  1 **small clove garlic,
     crushed**
  ⅛ **tsp. Dijon mustard**
  ⅓ **cup olive oil**
  1½ **tsps. Champagne
     vinegar
     Pinch of salt
     Freshly ground black
     pepper**
  8 **oz. smoked salmon, cut
     into ribbons ¼-inch by
     3-inch**
  4 **lobsters, 2 lbs. each,
     cooked, meat removed
     from shell, cut into
     julienne strips**
  4 **endive leaves, cut into
     julienne strips**
 20 **asparagus, cooked,
     peeled, cut into
     4-inch lengths**
  ½ **cup crème fraîche,
     optional**
  2 **Tbsps. caviar,
     domestic, optional**

Prepare a champagne dressing by combining the garlic, mustard, olive oil, champagne vinegar, salt and pepper in a small screw-top jar and shake vigorously to form an emulsion; adjust the seasoning to taste.

In a mixing bowl, place the smoked salmon, lobster and sliced endive. Gently toss with half of the champagne vinaigrette and set aside.

In a separate bowl, toss the asparagus in the remaining champagne vinaigrette.

Fan the asparagus out on the bottom of the plate. At the top of the asparagus, neatly place the salmon lobster salad, leaving room for the tips of the asparagus to be sticking out of the edge.

Mix crème fraîche with the caviar and neatly pour the mixture over the top of the asparagus.

John Halligan
Halcyon
RIHGA Royal Hotel
New York, New York

☆

Sweet Potato Salad

Cook sweet potatoes until done, but still firm. Plunge in ice water to stop cooking and drain well. Set aside.

To make the pickled pepper relish, place the green and red peppers and onions in a 2-quart non-reactive pot. Pour boiling water over and let stand 10 minutes. Add the vinegar, salt, sugar, celery seeds and chiles to the vegetables. Bring to boil and then simmer over low heat for 15 minutes.

Combine 1 cup of the relish, garlic and Dijon mustard in a bowl. Whisk in the olive oil and salt, pepper and Worcestershire sauce to taste.

Fold in the sweet potatoes and Italian parsley, then toss gently. This dish will keep well refrigerated for two days.

Serves 8
Preparation Time:
  45 Minutes

Per Serving:
  344 calories,
  2 g protein,
  38 g carbohydrates,
  20 g fat

  2 **lbs. sweet potatoes,**
    peeled, cut into
    ½ -inch chunks
  3 **green peppers, diced**
  1½ **cups red pepper, small**
    dice (about 4 large)
  1 **medium red onion,**
    chopped
  ¾ **cup cider vinegar**
  1½ **tsps. salt**
  ⅓ **cup sugar**
  ½ **tsp. celery seeds**
  2 **chipotle chiles, halved,**
    seeded
  1 **tsp. minced garlic**
  2 **Tbsps. Dijon mustard**
  ¾ **cup olive oil**
    Salt, pepper and
    Worcestershire sauce
    to taste
  ¼ **cup Italian parsley,**
    chopped

Ben Barker
Magnolia Grill
Durham, North Carolina

Szechuan Cabbage Salad

Serves 4
Preparation Time:
  10 Minutes
  (note marinating time)

Per Serving:
  141 calories,
  1 g protein,
  4 g carbohydrates,
  13 g fat

2 **Tbsps. Chinese chile paste**
2 **Tbsps. dark sesame oil**
2 **tsps. soy sauce**
¼ **cup rice wine vinegar**
2 **tsps. fresh ginger, chopped**
1 **garlic clove, finely chopped**
  Salt and pepper to taste
2 **Tbsps. corn oil**
½ **head red cabbage, very finely sliced**

 n a bowl, whisk together the chile paste, sesame oil, soy sauce, rice wine vinegar, ginger, garlic, salt, pepper and corn oil.

Toss the dressing with the cabbage in a large bowl and cover tightly.

Marinate the salad for 30 minutes to 1 hour. Serve with grilled or broiled meat or fish.

Clark Frasier
Mark Gaier
Arrows
Ogunquit, Maine

☆

Tuna Marinated in Sake with a Shiitake Salad

S lice tuna ¼-inch thick and into 1¼-inch pieces. Flatten between sheets of plastic wrap with a flat mallet until very thin. Marinate in sake. Set aside.

Prepare the salad by combining the mushrooms, carrot, onion, scallions and bok choy. In a separate bowl make the dressing by combining the vinegar, soy sauce, ginger and sesame oil. Toss shiitake salad ingredients with the dressing. Marinate for several minutes at room temperature or hours under refrigeration.

In a mixing bowl blend together the sour cream and wasabi powder and refrigerate.

To serve, the tuna and the shiitake salad can be piled separately on the same plate. The wasabi sour cream can be placed in a squeeze bottle and drizzled over the entire plate. The plate can be garnished with cucumber slices, pickled ginger, or sesame crackers.

Serves 4
Preparation Time:
  30 Minutes

Per Serving:
  184 calories,
  28 g protein,
  8 g carbohydrates,
  2 g fat

1 **lb. fresh ahi tuna**
4 **Tbsps. sake**
½ **lb. shiitake mushrooms, julienned**
1 **carrot, julienned**
1 **red onion, julienned**
2 **scallions, sliced thin on bias**
½ **cup bok choy, chiffonade**
½ **cup rice wine vinegar**
2 **Tbsps. soy sauce**
1 **tsp. ginger, grated**
1 **tsp. sesame oil**
½ **cup low-fat sour cream**
2 **tsps. wasabi powder**

Chris Needham
Trio Bistro & Bar
Tucson, Arizona

☆

Breads
and
Pizza

Apple Pizza

Make the pizza dough in a mixing bowl by combining the yeast, water and sugar. Let stand for 5 minutes. With a mixer fitted with a dough hook, or by hand, mix in salt, olive oil and the two flours. Knead until dough forms a ball and is smooth and elastic. Place in a mixing bowl and cover with a towel. Set aside in a warm place and let rise, about 20 minutes. Spray pizza pan or baking sheet with vegetable spray and sprinkle with cornmeal. Set aside.

After dough rises, transfer onto a floured board and knead well with hands. Divide and shape dough into two large balls. Use only one ball for this pizza. Using lightly floured rolling pin, spread and shape one ball of dough into a large circle, 14-inch in diameter. Transfer to a prepared pizza pan or baking sheet.

Place halved apples on a work surface and thinly slice crosswise. Fan the thin apple slices on the dough, starting with the outside edge, making a large ring. Working toward the center, fan the smaller circles of apple slices until all the dough is covered. Combine the sugar and cinnamon and sprinkle over apples. Bake for 20 to 25 minutes or until light golden brown.

In a small saucepan, combine the apricot preserves and orange liqueur. Over low heat, stir and warm the preserves until dissolved. Brush pizza with glaze. Cut into eight pie-shaped pieces and serve immediately.

Serves 8
Preparation Time:
1¼ Hours
Pre-heat oven to 350°

Per Serving:
180 calories,
3 g protein,
41 g carbohydrates,
1 g fat

1 Tbsp. active dry yeast
¾ cup tepid water
½ tsp. sugar or honey
1 tsp. Kosher salt
1 tsp. olive oil
¾ cup unbleached flour, white (plus flour to dust work surface)
½ cup whole wheat flour
1 Tbsp. cornmeal
4 golden delicious or Granny Smith apples, peeled, cored, halved
1 tsp. ground cinnamon
¼ cup white sugar
¼ cup apricot preserves, sugar-free
1 tsp. orange liqueur

Michel Stroot
Golden Door Health Resort
Escondido, California

★

97

Pizza Dough

**Yield: one 15-inch pizza or
two 9-inch pizzas
Preparation Time:
45 Minutes
Pre-heat oven to 500°**

Per Serving:
288 calories,
7 g protein,
45 g carbohydrates,
8 g fat

1½ tsp. active dry yeast
6 Tbsps. warm water
(110°)
6 Tbsps. milk
2 Tbsps. extra virgin
olive oil
1 Tbsp. fine cornmeal
½ tsp. salt
1 Tbsp. rye flour
1¾ cup unbleached white
flour
1 to 3 Tbsps. additional
flour for rolling the
dough

Dissolve the yeast in the warm water and set aside in a warm place for 3 to 4 minutes.

Meanwhile, combine the milk, oil, and cornmeal in a 1 qt. bowl. Add the yeast mixture, then the salt and rye flour; mix well. Gradually add the white flour, making a soft, workable dough. Turn out onto a lightly floured work surface and knead for about 5 minutes, sprinkling in a little flour as necessary to keep the dough from sticking to the surface. Put the dough into an oiled bowl and turn it once so the surface is coated with oil. Cover the bowl with a kitchen towel or plastic wrap and let the dough rise in a warm place until it has doubled in bulk, about 35 to 40 minutes.

To shape the pizza, first form the dough into one round ball or two equal-size smaller balls. Roll out on a floured surface, turning it regularly to keep a round shape. It should be about ⅛ inch thick, slightly thicker at the edges. Lay the dough on an oiled pizza pan. Cover with the topping you have chosen. Bake the pizza on its pan or slide it onto the heated pizza stone.

Annie Somerville
Greens
© Fields of Greens Cookbook
San Francisco, California

Non-Dairy Pizza Dough

Prepare and roll out the dough as directed on the preceding page.

To freeze: immediately after mixing the dough, form it into one or two balls and wrap tightly in two layers of plastic wrap. When you're ready to use the dough, thaw it in the refrigerator overnight, or set it in a warm place for 2 or 3 hours. Roll out as directed.

Brush the rolled-out pizza dough with this garlic-infused oil before spreading on the topping—the garlic oil adds extra garlic flavor and forms a seal that helps protect the crust from moist toppings. To make it, finely chop a clove or two of garlic and cover generously with olive oil. Store garlic oil in a sealed container in the refrigerator and use it to sauté or season other dishes.

**Yield: one 15-inch pizza or
two 9-inch pizzas**
**Preparation Time:
45 Minutes**
Pre-heat oven to 500°

Per Serving:
422 calories,
1 g protein,
3 g carbohydrates,
78 g fat

1½ tsps. active dry yeast
10 Tbsp. warm water
(110°)
¼ cup extra virgin olive oil
1 Tbsp. fine cornmeal
½ tsp. salt
1 Tbsp. rye flour
1¾ cup unbleached white flour
1 to 3 Tbsps. Additional flour for rolling the dough

Annie Somerville
Greens
© Fields of Greens Cookbook
San Francisco, California

Greek Pizza with Spinach, Feta Cheese, and Rosemary

Yield: one 15-inch or
  two 9-inch pizzas
Preparation Time:
  30 Minutes
Pre-heat oven to 500°

Per Serving:
  469 calories,
  28 g protein,
  9 g carbohydrates,
  35 g fat

1 Tbsp. extra virgin
   olive oil
½ medium-size red onion,
   thinly sliced
   Salt & pepper
2 garlic cloves, finely
   chopped
1 large bunch of spinach,
   stems removed
1 tsp. minced lemon zest
   Pizza Dough, ready to
   roll out, recipes on
   pages 98, 99
6 Kalamata olives, pitted
   and coarsely chopped
1½ cups feta cheese,
   crumbled
1½ cups grated mozzarella
   cheese, grated
3 Tbsps. Parmesan
   cheese, grated
1 tsp. chopped fresh
   rosemary

H eat 2 tsps. of olive oil in a sauté pan. Add the red onion, ¼ teaspoon salt, and a few pinches of pepper; sauté over medium heat for 4 to 5 minutes, until tender. Add half of the garlic and sauté for 1 minute. Transfer to a bowl.

Heat the remaining teaspoon of olive oil in the pan. Wilt the spinach over high heat with ¼ teaspoon salt, a few pinches of pepper, and the remaining garlic. When the spinach is wilted but still bright green, in about 1 minute, remove it from the pan and place it in a strainer to cool. Squeeze out the excess moisture with your hands, then coarsely chop and toss with the lemon zest.

Roll out the dough and place it on a lightly oiled pizza pan and brush with the garlic oil. Spread the onion on the dough, followed by the spinach. Sprinkle the olives over the spinach, follow with the crumbled feta, then add the mozzarella cheese.

Bake the pizza, in the pan or on a Pre-heated pizza stone, for 8 to 12 minutes, until the crust is golden and crisp. Remove it from the oven and sprinkle with the Parmesan cheese and fresh rosemary.

COOKING SECRET: You can substitute chard for the spinach; just be sure it's tender and well seasoned.

Annie Somerville
Greens
© Fields of Greens Cookbook
San Francisco, California

★

Lemon Pepper Foccacia

In a large mixing bowl combine the flour, yeast, water and salt. Knead for 10 minutes. Allow dough to rest covered with a cloth for 10 minutes.

Roll the dough out on a floured table to a 14-inch circle with ½-inch thickness. Place the dough on a lightly oiled sheet pan and brush dough with half of the olive oil. Sprinkle with fresh rosemary, and generous amounts of freshly milled black pepper. Place the lemon slices evenly over the bread. Cover with a cloth and allow to rise for 20 to 25 minutes in a warm place.

With fingers spread apart, lightly make indentations into the bread. This allows the olive oil to stay on the bread.

Bake in a preheated oven at 425° or until bread is golden brown and sounds hollow when lifted and tapped on the bottom, about 20 minutes.

Remove from the oven and brush with the remaining olive oil. Sprinkle with Parmesan cheese if desired.

Serves 12
Preparation Time:
1½ Hours
Pre-heat oven to 425°

Per Serving:
144 calories,
3 g protein,
12 g carbohydrates,
9 g fat

1½ **cup bread flour**
¼ **oz. dried yeast**
¾ **cup cold water**
Pinch of salt
½ **cup extra virgin olive oil**
1 **Tbsp. fresh rosemary, chopped**
½ **lemon thinly sliced, deseeded**
2 **Tbsps. Parmesan cheese, grated, optional**
Black pepper, freshly ground

Kevin Taylor
Zenith American Grill
Denver, Colorado

★

Viennese Five-Grain Bread

Yield: 2 loaves
Preparation Time:
1½ Hours
Pre-heat the oven to 350°

Per Serving:
222 calories,
8 g protein,
43 g carbohydrates,
2 g fat

4½ tsp. active dry yeast,
  2 packages
3½ cups warm water (110°)
1 cup unbleached white
  flour
1½ cups dark rye flour
1½ tsp. gluten flour
½ cup rye flakes
3 Tbsps. flax seed
3 Tbsps. sesame seed
3 Tbsps. sunflower seed
3 Tbsps. rolled oats
3 Tbsps. millet
4½ Tbsps. dark sulfured
  molasses
2 tsps. sea salt
4 cups unbleached white
  flour
1 tablespoon each rolled
  oats, sesame seed, flax
  seed, and hulled
  sunflower seed
1 egg white beaten with
  1 teaspoon water

Combine the yeast and 3/4 cup water in a medium-size bowl. Stir to dissolve the yeast and let sit for 10 minutes. Stir in the unbleached white flour until well incorporated and let sit for one hour. This is known as the sponge.

Combine the sponge and 2¾ cups of the warm water in a large bowl and stir to break up the sponge. Stir in all of the ingredients except for the sea salt and 4 cups unbleached white flour. Add the salt and one cup unbleached white flour. Stir until the ingredients are moistened, then continue adding the flour one cup at a time. (It may be necessary to knead in the last of the flour by hand.)

Turn the dough out onto a lightly floured work surface and knead it for 10 to 15 minutes, adding more flour as needed to keep the dough from sticking, until the dough is smooth and elastic. The dough should feel tacky and moist throughout the kneading. Keep track of how much flour you're adding as you knead the dough; try not to use more than a total of 4½ cups.

Place the dough in an oiled bowl, turning to coat the surface with oil. Cover with a damp towel or plastic wrap and let rise at room temperature for about one hour, until doubled in size.

Lightly oil two 8½×4-inch loaf pans. (The bread can be baked in standard 9×5-inch loaf pans, but the smaller pans will yield a loftier loaf.) Turn the dough onto the work surface, punch it down, and divide in half. Form into two loaves and place in the oiled pans. Cover the pans loosely with a damp towel and allow to rise for one hour, until doubled in size.

Combine the topping ingredients. Brush the loaves with the egg white and water and sprinkle with the topping. Bake for 40 to 45 minutes, until the loaves sound hollow when tapped on the bottom. Remove from the pans and transfer to a rack to cool.

Annie Somerville
Greens
© Fields of Greens Cookbook
San Francisco, California

★

Fish and Shellfish

Baked Pumpkin-Seed Crusted Bass, Coriander Rice

Walnut-Crusted Salmon

Ginger Tuna Tartare

Grilled Rockfish with Vegetables

Grilled Mediterranean Swordfish

Hickory Roasted Black Sea Bass

Paella with Prawns, Lobster, Monkfish and Clams

Pecan-Crusted Red Snapper with Corn Tomatillo Salsa

Pinenut-Crusted Red Snapper with Balsamic Vinegar Sauce

Poached Rainbow Trout with Corn Ragout

Poached Salmon with Baby Vegetables

Salmon and Shrimp Papillote, Indian Dahl Ginger Sauce

Salt-Crusted Fish

Sardine Filets on Potatoes with Rosemary Vinaigrette

Sautéed Shrimp on Linguine with Cajun Sauce

Sea Bass with Broccoli in Red Wine

Seared Salmon with Couscous and Citrus

Seared Tuna with Avocado Vinaigrette and Melon Salsa

Shellfish, Corn and Potato Johnnycakes

Spiced Mahi Mahi with Sweet Pepper Gazpacho

Tuna Steak with Wild Spring Vegetables

Wok-Charred Maine Lobster

★

Baked Pumpkin Seed-Crusted Sea Bass with Coriander Rice and Orange Pineapple Salsa

Serves 6
Preparation Time:
  45 Minutes
Pre-heat oven to 350°

Per Serving:
  370 calories,
  34 g protein,
  9 g carbohydrates,
  21 g fat

  6 sea bass filets, 5 oz.
     each
  8 Tbsps. olive oil
     Salt and ground white
     pepper to taste
  ⅓ cup basmati rice
  ⅓ cup water
  ½ tsp. coriander seeds,
     crushed
  1 Tbsp. currants, soaked
     in water
  1 Tbsp. Italian parsley,
     rough chopped
  2 Tbsps. lime juice
  ¼ cup pumpkin seeds,
     toasted, crushed
     Orange pineapple salsa,
     recipe follows

R inse fish and season with olive oil, salt and pepper to taste. Refrigerate.

In a small pot, add rice, water and salt. Bring to a simmer and cover. Cook until rice is tender, approximately 12 to 15 minutes. Remove from heat and add coriander seeds, currants, parsley and lime juice. Set aside.

Place a cast iron or heavy-bottom skillet over moderate heat. Pour in 2 Tbsps. olive oil and sear seasoned fish filets on both sides. Remove from skillet and spoon 2 Tbsps. of pumpkin seeds over the top of each fillet. Place in a 350° oven for 6 to 8 minutes.

Serve with orange and pineapple salsa.

Charles Saunders
Eastside Oyster Bar & Grill
Sonoma, California

☆

Orange and Pineapple Salsa

n a non-reactive mixing bowl, combine all the ingredients.

Yields: 1½ cups
Preparation Time:
   15 Minutes

Per Serving:
   151 calories,
   1 g protein,
   17 g carbohydrates,
   9 g fat

1 **pineapple, halved,**
   grilled, finely diced
1 **red bell pepper, roasted,**
   peeled, finely diced
2 **oranges, purée in a**
   blender
½ **bunch basil, chiffonade**
4 **Tbsps. red onion,**
   minced
1 **jalapeño, deseeded and**
   finely diced
¼ **cup orange juice**
4 **Tbsps. virgin olive oil**

Charles Saunders
Eastside Oyster Bar & Grill
Sonoma, California
☆

Walnut Crusted Salmon

Serves 4
Preparation Time:
   30 Minutes
Pre-heat oven to 350°

Per Serving:
   614 calories,
   89 g protein,
   8 g carbohydrates,
   34 g fat

½ **cup walnuts**
1½ **tsps. chopped basil or**
   ½ **tsp. dried**
4 **salmon filets or steaks**
1 **cup low-fat buttermilk**
   Salt and pepper to taste

G rind the walnuts and basil in a food processor. Set aside.

Dip the salmon into the buttermilk and then the walnut basil mixture. Season with salt and pepper.

Cook on an oiled baking sheet for 12 to 15 minutes or until done or sauté in a medium-heated skillet until golden on each side, about 6 minutes per side.

Clarence Cohen
Pitty Pat's Porch
Rutherford, Georgia

☆

Gingered Tuna Tartare

sing a very sharp knife, carefully cut tuna into small ⅛-inch pieces. Place tuna into a glass or non-reactive metal bowl.

Add the oil, vinegar, ginger and jalapeño. Mix well and season to taste with salt and pepper.

Serve tartar on a bed of mixed baby greens. Drizzle with extra virgin olive oil and sherry vinegar.

Serves 4
Preparation Time:
   15 Minutes

Per Serving:
   254 calories,
   40 g protein,
   1 g carbohydrates,
   8 g fat

1½ lbs. fresh, top-quality tuna
 2 Tbsps. olive oil
 2 Tbsps. sherry vinegar
   4-inch piece of ginger, peeled, minced
 1 jalapeño, seeded, ribbed, minced
   Salt and black pepper
 2 cups baby salad greens

Michael Cron
Il Monello
New York, New York

Grilled Rockfish with Vegetables

Serves 4
Preparation Time:
35 Minutes

Per Serving:
285 calories,
33 g protein,
4 g carbohydrates,
14 g fat

4 **rockfish fillets, 6 to 8 oz.**
each
Sea salt and freshly
ground pepper to taste
4 **Tbsps. extra virgin**
olive oil
3 **shallots, chopped**
2 **carrots, peeled, diced**
1 **bulb fennel, diced**
1 **red bell pepper, diced**
2 **Tbsps. capers 1 hard**
boiled egg, chopped
Juice of 1 lemon
2 **Tbsps. chives**

Season the filets with a pinch of sea salt and freshly ground pepper. Brush with 1 Tbsp. olive oil.

Heat 3 Tbsps. olive oil in a sauté pan until hot. Add the shallots for 1 minute then add the rest of the vegetables and sauté for 2 more minutes. Remove from heat and let the vegetables cool.

In a mixing bowl, combine the capers, chopped egg and lemon juice. Add the cooled vegetables. Refrigerate the vegetable mixture while grilling the fish.

Place the fish on a hot grill for 3 to 4 minutes on each side.

To serve, arrange the vegetables in a circle in the middle of each serving plate. Place the filets skin up. Sprinkle with chop chives.

Bruno Fortini
Bistrot Lepic
Washington, DC

☆

Grilled Mediterranean Swordfish

Brush swordfish with olive oil and season with salt and pepper. Refrigerate.

In a medium-sized sauté pan on moderate heat, warm 2 Tbsps. olive oil. Add the onions, fennel and 1 Tbsp. garlic and sauté until clear. Add the artichokes, olives, and tomatoes. Add the herbs, wine and stock to the pan. Season with salt and pepper. Cook the ingredients only long enough to heat thoroughly. Set aside.

Cut the potatoes lengthwise into 6 pieces. Toss the potatoes with 1 to 2 Tbsps. garlic, rosemary and 1 to 2 Tbsps. olive oil and set aside until the grill is ready.

Place the fish in the center of the grill to gain maximum exposure to the heat of the grill and cook to desired doneness.

Place the potatoes on the perimeter of the grill to gain color but not char. For each serving, pour the broth into a shallow soup bowl. Place two pieces of the potatoes on the broth and the third criss-cross. Lay the swordfish at an angle against the potatoes.

Serves 6
Preparation Time:
  45 Minutes

Per Serving:
  554 calories,
  38 g protein,
  34 g carbohydrates,
  28 g fat

  4 Tbsps. olive oil
     Sea salt and ground
     white pepper to taste
  6 center-cut swordfish, 6
     oz. each
  4 Tbsps. olive oil
  1 cup onion, peeled,
     sliced thin
  1 cup fennel, sliced thin
  3 Tbsps. garlic, chopped
  2 cups baby artichokes,
     halved
 24 Kalamata olives
  ½ cup tomatoes, diced
  2 Tbsps. fresh basil,
     roughly chopped
  2 Tbsps. fresh oregano,
     roughly chopped
  ¼ cup Sauvignon Blanc
  ¼ cup fish stock or water
  3 russet potatoes, baked,
     cool
  2 Tbsps. rosemary, finely
     chopped

Charles Saunders
Eastside Oyster Bar & Grill
Sonoma, California

Hickory Roasted Black Sea Bass

Serves 4
Preparation Time:
   30 Minutes
Pre-heat oven to 350°

Per Serving:
   545 calories,
   43 g protein,
   43 g carbohydrates,
   24 g fat

4 **sea bass filets, 6 to 7 oz.**
   each,
½ **cup soaked hickory**
   chips
1 **cup wild mushrooms:**
   chanterelle, shiitake,
   portobello, etc.
2 **cups hot vegetable**
   broth, enriched with
   mushroom stems, herb
   stems, white wine
4 **cups mashed potatoes**
¼ **cup green beans,**
   trimmed, blanched
½ **cup walnuts, toasted,**
   optional
½ **cup low-fat crème**
   fraîche
1 **Tbsp. fresh chopped**
   thyme
1 **Tbsp. lemon juice**

 auté sea bass on one side. Turn filets and lower heat by half. Add hickory chips and cover pan with a lid, then place in oven and roast for 3 minutes.

Heat mushrooms in broth. Set aside.

Place portion of mashed potatoes on each plate. Spoon stock, mushrooms and green beans around potatoes. Place filets on top of potatoes. Sprinkle walnuts about plate.

In a mixing bowl combine the crème fraîche with the thyme and lemon juice. Place small dollop of thyme crème fraîche on each filet.

Clark Frasier
Mark Gaier
Arrows Restaurant
Ogunquit, Maine

☆

New England Halibut Fish Bake

S core the filets at 1-inch intervals and less than $\frac{1}{16}$-inch deep on the skin side to avoid curling when cooked.

Season lightly with salt and pepper.

The moment before sautéing, dredge the fish lightly in the flour and sprinkle with fresh thyme.

Heat the sauté pan with the oil. Sauté the filets until golden on one side. Turn the filets over and finish cooking in 375° oven for approximately 10 minutes.

Serves 6
Preparation Time:
   15 Minutes
Pre-heat oven to 375°

Per Serving:
   544 calories,
   87 g protein,
   15 g carbohydrates,
   11 g fat

6 **halibut steaks, ½-inch thick**
   Salt and freshly ground white pepper to taste
1 **cup flour**
1 **Tbsp. fresh thyme, minced**
1 **Tbsp. olive oil**

Paul O'Connell
Providence
Brookline, Massachusetts

Paella With Prawns, Lobster, Monkfish and Clams

Serves 4
Preparation Time:
  One Hour

Per Serving:
  743 calories,
  92 g protein,
  55 g carbohydrates,
  14 g fat

1 cup long grain basmati
  rice
2¼ cups vegetable broth or
  water
1 bay leaf
2 tsps. olive oil or canola
  oil
2 garlic cloves, minced
½ onion, diced
2 celery stalks, diced
1 tsp. fennel seeds
8 medium prawns,
  peeled, deveined
4 oz. lobster tails,
  cut in 1-inch pieces
½ lb. white fish filets,
  monkfish preferred, cut
  in 1-inch pieces
8 clams with shells,
  scrubbed ½ tsp.
  saffron threads
  Freshly ground black
  pepper to taste
¼ cup dry white wine
1 cup fresh or frozen
  peas, cooked
2 tsps. lemon zest
½ cup fresh parsley,
  minced

n a medium-sized saucepan, combine the rice, vegetable stock and bay leaf. Simmer, covered for about 35 minutes.

In a wide-bottomed stock pot, heat olive oil over medium heat. Add the garlic, onion, celery and fennel seeds. Stir and sauté for 2 to 3 minutes. Add the prawns, lobster, monkfish and clams. Sprinkle in the saffron, black pepper and white wine over the seafood. Let simmer, covered for about 5 to 7 minutes, until seafood is cooked.

Use a kitchen fork to mix peas and lemon zest into the cooked rice. Spread the rice-pea mixture evenly over the seafood. Shake the pot to integrate all the ingredients. Sprinkle with parsley and serve.

Michel Stroot
Golden Door Health Resort
Escondido, California

★

Pecan-Crusted Red Snapper with Corn Tomatillo Salsa

P repare the crust for the fish by combining the pecans, graham cracker crumbs, sugar and spices. Place three containers side by side, one each for the flour, egg and pecan mixture. Season fish with salt and pepper. Dust fish with flour, then dip in egg, and finally coat with nuts. Set fish aside.

Make the salsa by mixing together the corn, tomatillo, red pepper, cilantro, lemon juice, olive oil, scallions and onions in a large mixing bowl. Adjust seasonings to your taste.

Heat a sauté pan over medium heat with 2 Tbsps. olive oil. Add the fish and sauté until crisp, 2 to 3 minutes on each side.

Drain the fish on paper towels, then transfer to heated plates and top with salsa.

Serves 4
Preparation Time:
  25 Minutes

Per Serving:
  613 calories,
  53 g protein,
  30 g carbohydrates,
  32 g fat

8 red snapper filets,
  8 oz. each
2 cups roasted pecans,
  chopped fine
½ cup graham cracker
  crumbs
3 Tbsps. sugar, optional
2 Tbsps. combined cumin,
  coriander and cayenne
  powder (equal parts)
½ cup all-purpose flour
4 eggs, beaten
  Salt and pepper to taste
1½ cups fresh or frozen
  cooked corn
1½ cups tomatillo, diced
¾ cup red pepper, diced
1 bunch cilantro, chopped
  Juice of 1 lemon or lime
3 Tbsps. extra virgin
  olive oil
1 bunch scallions, sliced
  (green part only)
1 small red onion, diced

Fred Sabo
Tropica
New York, New York

☆

Pine Nut-Crusted Red Snapper with a Balsamic Vinegar Sauce

Serves 4
Preparation Time:
45 Minutes
Pre-heat oven to 400°

Per Serving:
703 calories,
87 g protein,
133 g carbohydrates,
69 g fat

2 cups pine nuts
2 cups bread crumbs
¼ cup parsley, chopped
4 cups balsamic vinegar
10 plum tomatoes, cut in half
½ cup brown sugar
4 snapper filets, cleaned
  Flour
4 eggs, beaten
  Cooking oil
½ lb. spinach, sautéed
  Parsley, chopped for garnish

repare a crust by processing the nuts quickly in a food processor. Add the bread crumbs and parsley. Pulse, then set aside.

Prepare the sauce by combining the balsamic vinegar, tomatoes and brown sugar in a saucepan. Reduce by ⅔ over low heat. Strain, pushing solids with a ladle or spoon.

Dredge each filet in flour; shake off excess. Dip meat side of filet in egg, then pine nut mixture.

In a sauté pan heat oil, then add the filets, crust side down. When the crust is browned, turn the fillets over and cook skin side briefly. Press flat with a spatula if skin starts to curl.

Finish cooking in a 400° oven for approximately 12 to 15 minutes.

To serve, place a portion of the spinach in the center of each of four plates. Spoon sauce to cover plate around spinach. Place one filet over spinach on each plate. Sprinkle with chopped parsley if desired.

Michael Cron
Il Monello
New York, New York

☆

Poached Rainbow Trout with Corn Ragout

Stuff trout with thin slices of lemon and thyme sprigs.

In a sauté pan, add ¼ cup white wine, ½ cup stock and ¼ cup water. Season trout and add to sauté pan.

Cook in 450° oven for 8 to 10 minutes.

Add olive oil to sauté pan. When pan is hot, add the corn. Once the corn browns, add the garlic and trout. Add 1 cup stock, sage and parsley.

Serve immediately.

Serves 8
Preparation Time:
  30 Minutes
Pre-heat oven to 450°

Per Serving:
  245 calories,
  36 g protein,
  7 g carbohydrates,
  6 g fat

8 trout, 6 oz. each
½ lemon, sliced thin
2 sprigs thyme
¼ cup white wine
1½ cup fish, vegetable or chicken stock
¼ cup water
  Kosher salt and fresh ground black pepper
1 tsp. olive oil
1 cup fresh corn
½ tsp. garlic, chopped
½ tsp. sage, chopped
1 tsp. parsley, chopped rough

Marion Gillcrist
The Double A
Santa Fe, New Mexico

Poached Salmon with Spring Baby Vegetables

Serves 4
Preparation Time:
   20 Minutes

Per Serving:
   599 calories,
   79 g protein,
   5 g carbohydrates,
   25 g fat

½ lb. assortment of
   cleaned baby vegetables
   in season (turnips,
   carrots, zucchini,
   squash, etc.)
1 pt. water
¼ cup dry vermouth
1 tsp. cracked black
   pepper
2 tsps. thyme
4 salmon filets

Blanch baby vegetables in simmering water for 2 to 3 minutes or until tender. Cool the vegetables under running water.

In a shallow pot bring the water, vermouth, peppercorns and thyme to a simmer. Place the salmon in the liquid. Cook until rare, then add the vegetables to the pot. Cover and cook salmon to desired temperature. Continue cooking vegetables until heated through.

To serve, place the salmon filets in 4 different bowls and top with vegetables.

Christopher Gross
Christopher's
Phoenix, Arizona

Salmon and Shrimp Papillote with Indian Dahl and Ginger Sauce

Combine the salmon, shrimp, cilantro, 1 Tbsp. garlic, Mirin, tamari, sesame oil and ½ cup vegetable broth in a small mixing bowl and let marinate, refrigerated, for about 2 hours.

In a medium-sized saucepan, heat the oil over medium heat. Add 1 Tbsp. garlic, onion and jalapeño and sauté until softened. Stir in tomato, lentils, curry powder and cumin. Add 2¼ cups vegetable broth. Let simmer for 25 minutes or until lentils are soft. Mix dahl with a wooden spatula to a purée consistency, adding more broth or water, if necessary. Set aside and keep warm.

Soak the rice papers in cold water for 2 to 3 minutes or until softened and flexible. Thoroughly dampen a work surface with water and lay the soaked rice papers on the work surface. Arrange the salmon and shrimp in the center of the paper, sprinkle with some marinade, and fold the rice paper around the salmon and shrimp, like a letter.

Place the wrappers on a nonstick surface folded side down. Add a few tablespoons water or vegetable broth. Cover with plastic wrap and refrigerate until ready to bake.

Before baking, ladle ½ cup heated vegetable broth or fish stock over the salmon. Bake covered, in 350° oven, for about 12 to 15 minutes or until done. To serve, place the papillote next to the dahl and ladle with the ginger sauce (recipe follows.) Serve with steamed asparagus, red bell peppers and carrots, sprinkled with chopped chives.

Michel Stroot
Golden Door Health Resort
Escondido, California

Serves 4
Preparation Time: 45 Min.
(note marinating time)
Pre-heat oven to 350°

Per Serving:
353 calories, 28 g protein,
33 g carbohydrates,
12 g fat

½ **lb. salmon filets, 4 filets**
4 large shrimp,
1½ **oz. each, peeled, deveined, butterflied**
2 **Tbsps. cilantro leaves, chopped**
2 **Tbsp. minced garlic cloves**
2 **Tbsps. Mirin (sweet sake)**
2 **Tbsps. low-sodium tamari**
1 **tsp. toasted sesame oil**
3 **cups vegetable broth**
2 **Tbsps. canola oil**
½ **medium white onion, minced**
1 **jalapeño chile pepper, seeded, minced**
1 **large tomato, diced**
1 **cup red lentils, rinsed**
1 **Tbsp. curry powder**
2 **tsps. ground cumin**
Freshly ground black pepper to taste
4 **rice sheets or rice paper, 8-inch in diameter**
Ginger sauce, recipe follows

Ginger Sauce

Preparation Time:
  10 Minutes

Per Serving:
  27 calories,
  1 g protein,
  6 g carbohydrates

**2 tsps. fresh ginger root,
  minced**
**1 tsp. fresh garlic cloves,
  minced**
1 Tbsp. fresh lime juice
1 Tbsp. Miso, light barley
1 Tbsp. fructose, or honey
2 to 3 drops chile sauce
¼ cup vegetable stock

I n a blender, combine the ginger root, garlic, lime juice, Miso, fructose or honey and chile sauce. Blend to a smooth consistency.

Before serving add the vegetable stock.

Michel Stroot
Golden Door Health Resort
Escondido, California

☆

Salt-Crusted Fish

In a sheet pan, place ¼ inch of salt. Place fish on salt and cover with remaining salt so that fish is completely covered.

Place fish in a hot oven and cook for approximately 50 minutes. You can check the temperature in the thickest part of fish near the gills. The temperature should be 145°.

In a sauce pot, bring the water, 2 Tbsps. olive oil and 1 tablespoon of salt. to a boil and add the cleaned leeks, split in half. Blanch until green and tender.

In a separate sauce pot add the 3 Tbsps. olive oil, then add the crushed pepper, lemon juice and rosemary, turn off, let steep.

When fish is at 145° internal temperature, crack off the salt crust with a fork, run around the back bone from head to tail cutting the skin. This will allow the skin to be pulled back. Do not let fish flesh touch salt. Remove the flesh.

On a hot serving plate, place the leeks in a decorative manner, then garnish flesh with hot olive oil, one piece of rosemary and ½ lemon.

Serves 4
Preparation Time:
1½ Hours
Pre-heat over to 400°

Per Serving:
674 calories,
82 g protein,
14 g carbohydrates,
30 g fat

1 **whole firm-fleshed fish, approx. 4 lbs., gutted with gills removed, rinsed Kosher salt**
1 **qt. water**
½ **cup olive oil**
2 **leeks**
2 **Tbsps. black pepper, fresh cracked, to taste**
  Juice of 2 lemons
4 **pieces rosemary**
½ **lemon as garnish**

Jamie Shannon
Commander's Palace
New Orleans, Louisiana

☆

Sardine Filets on Potatoes with Rosemary Vinaigrette

Serves 4
Preparation Time:
45 Minutes (note refrigeration time)

Per Serving:
431 calories,
4 g protein,
24 g carbohydrates,
36 g fat

6 **fresh sardines**
  Salt and pepper to taste
½ **cup + 2 Tbsps. olive oil**
1 **onion, sliced**
1 **bunch thyme**
2 **large baking potatoes, diced**
1 **bunch basil, chopped**
2 **shallots, chopped fine**
1 **tsp. balsamic vinegar**
1 **bunch chives, chopped fine**
10 **black olives, oil cured, chopped**
2 **tomatoes, diced**

F ilet the sardines with a sharp knife by cutting off the head and running the knife down both sides of the backbone (or ask the fishmonger to filet and clean the fish for you). What you should have is 12 filets of semi-boneless fish.

Place the sardines on a sheet pan, skin side down and lightly season with salt and pepper.

In a sauté pan, heat 2 Tbsps. olive oil over medium heat. Place the filets skin side up and cook for 2 minutes or until fish is cooked through. Don't turn the fish skin side down. The sardine skin is a beautiful silver-blue and when you cook the sardine on the skin it generally shrinks and tears.

Place sliced onions on a clean sheet pan and top with thyme.

With a spatula, carefully remove the cooked filet and place on top of the onions, skin side up. Allow the filets to cool in the refrigerator, then pour ¼ cup olive oil over the filets before covering them with wax paper or foil. The filets will keep up to 7 days in the refrigerator.

Cook the potatoes in salted water until soft. Remove from heat and purée with ¼ cup olive oil in a blender. When potatoes have cooled, add the basil, shallots and balsamic vinegar.

Place the potato mixture into a pastry bag and pipe out the basil potatoes the length of each sardine filet, skin side down.

To serve, lay the sardine filet skin side up on top of the potatoes. Discard the onion and thyme. Sprinkle the filets with black olives, chives and tomatoes. Drizzle with rosemary vinaigrette.

Cal Stamenov
Highlands Inn, Pacific's Edge
Carmel, California

☆

Sautéed Shrimp on Linguine with Cajun Sauce

I n a saucepan over medium-low heat sauté the peppers, carrots, celery and onions in olive oil. When vegetables are cooked through add 2 chopped shallots, 2 chopped garlic cloves and jalapeño.

Add white wine, chopped and puréed tomatoes, stock, and salt and pepper to taste. Keep warm.

In a sauté pan that is lightly oiled, quickly sauté the remaining shallots and garlic. Add the shrimp and sauté until heated through. Finish with chopped parsley, thyme, tarragon and basil.

To serve, place shrimp on top of pasta and drizzle with sauce.

Serves 4
Preparation Time:
  45 Minutes

Per Serving:
  515 calories,
  43 g protein,
  42 g carbohydrates,
  14 g fat

3 each, red, yellow and green peppers, diced
4 carrots, diced
1 bunch celery, diced
2 onions, diced
2 Tbsps. olive oil
4 shallots, chopped
4 garlic cloves, chopped
1 Tbsp. jalapeño, minced
1 cup white wine
8 cups, peeled, seeded, chopped tomatoes
1 can purée Italian plum tomatoes,
6 to 8 cups fish stock
1 Tbsp. canola oil
1½ lbs. large shrimp, cleaned, cooked
  Salt and pepper to taste
1 lb. linguini, cooked parsley, chopped thyme, chopped tarragon, chopped basil, chopped

Melissa Homann
Sarabeth's
New York, New York

✬

Sea Bass with Broccoli in Red Wine

Serves 4
Preparation Time:
 30 Minutes
Pre-heat oven to 375°

Per Serving:
 485 calories,
 44 g protein,
 6 g carbohydrates,
 16 g fat

3 Tbsps. extra virgin
 olive oil
4 sea bass filets, skin on,
 8 oz. each
 Salt and pepper to taste
2 garlic cloves, peeled
½ lb. broccoli, cleaned
4 leaves fresh sage
2 Tbsp. shallots, peeled,
 finely chopped
1 Tbsp. sweet butter,
 optional
¾ cup red wine

S pread oil on each filet and salt and pepper to taste. Roast in oven at 375° for 7 minutes.

Lightly sauté the garlic in 1 Tbsp. olive oil. Add the broccoli, salt and pepper to taste and cover. Cook at medium flame until softened. Set aside.

Brown the shallots in butter. Add the wine, salt and pepper to taste and reduce to ⅓. Strain.

To serve, place the broccoli in the middle of a platter, set the fish on top, skin up, and cover half of each fish with the wine sauce.

Michele Orsino
Ciao Europa
New York, New York

★

Seared Salmon with Couscous and Citrus in a Sesame Seed Vinaigrette

Marinate salmon in olive oil, 1 cup orange juice, coriander seeds, black peppercorns and chopped soft herbs overnight.

Sear on both sides until medium rare.

In a large saucepan bring to boil the stock, ½ cup orange juice, sugar and butter. Stir together couscous and cinnamon, then pour hot liquid over and stir. Cover with plastic wrap and let sit 10 minutes. Season to taste. Stir in cucumber.

Serve the salmon on a bed of couscous with the sesame seed vinaigrette.

Serves 4
Preparation Time:
   30 Minutes (note marinating time)

Per Serving:
   602 calories,
   70 g protein,
   49 g carbohydrates,
   11 g fat

   4 **salmon steaks or filets, 4 oz. each**
   2 **Tbsps. olive oil**
1½ **cup orange juice**
      Coriander seeds
      Black peppercorns Soft herbs of choice, chopped
   ½ **cup chicken stock**
   ¼ **tsp. brown sugar**
   1 **Tbsp. butter**
   1 **cup couscous**
   ⅛ **tsp. cinnamon**
      Salt & pepper to taste
   ¼ **cucumber, seeded, cubed**
      Sesame seed vinaigrette, recipe follows

Rick Tramonto
Brasserie T
Chicago, Illinois

★

Sesame Seed Vinaigrette

Yield: 1½ cups
Preparation Time:
  15 Minutes

Per Serving:
  320 calories,
  2 g protein,
  8 g carbohydrates,
  31 g fat

1 lime, zest and juice
1 orange, zest and juice
¼ tsp. ginger, grated
1 small garlic clove,
   minced
1 Tbsp. soy sauce
½ cup rice wine vinegar
½ cup canola oil
½ cup red bell pepper,
   chopped
1 small yellow bell
   pepper, chopped
1 bunch scallions, sliced
¼ cup sesame seeds,
   toasted
   Assorted citrus sections

 or the vinaigrette, in a mixing bowl, whisk together the juices, zest, ginger, garlic, soy sauce, vinegar and oil.

Stir in the vegetable, sesame seeds and citrus sections.

Rick Tramonto
Brasserie T
Chicago, Illinois

★

Seared Tuna with Avocado Vinaigrette and Melon Salsa

Boat each tuna steak with cracked pepper. In a hot sauté pan or wok with olive oil sear the steaks for approximately 1 to 2 minutes on each side. Remove from heat.

In a mixer or food processor blend the avocado, serrano peppers, lime juice and cilantro until smooth. Slowly drizzle the olive oil into the mixture until fully incorporated. Season with salt. If vinaigrette is too thick thin with water.

To serve, drizzle the avocado vinaigrette on a warm plate and then slice the tuna on the bias and fan on top of the vinaigrette. Spoon the melon salsa on top of the tuna and garnish with lime wedges.

Melon Salsa

Combine all the ingredients, allowing the flavors to blend for at least 20 minutes before serving.

Kevin Taylor
Zenith American Grill
Denver, Colorado

★

Serves 4
Preparation Time:
  30 Minutes

Per Serving:
  774 calories,
  41 g protein,
  11 g carbohydrates,
  63 g fat

4 **Tuna steaks, 6 oz.,**
    ½-inch thick
¼ **cup cracked black**
    pepper
1 **Tbsp. olive oil**
1 **ripe avocado**
3 **serrano peppers**
4 **Tbsps. lime juice**
½ **cup cilantro leaves**
1 **cup olive oil**
    Salt to taste

Melon Salsa
1 **cup diced mixed melon:**
    crenshaw, cantaloupe,
    honeydew, Persian
⅓ **cup diced bell peppers:**
    red, yellow and green
2 **Tbsps. cilantro leaves,**
    chopped
1 **Tbsp. honey**
2 **serrano peppers, finely**
    diced
    Juice of 2 limes
    Salt to taste

Shellfish, Corn and Potato Johnnycakes

Serves 6
Preparation Time:
  30 Minutes

Per Serving:
  260 calories,
  19 g protein,
  33 g carbohydrates,
  5 g fat

¾ lb. favorite shellfish:
  crab, shrimp or scallops
½ cup onions, finely diced
1 Tbsp. garlic, minced
1 Tbsp. olive oil
2 whole medium eggs
⅔ cup milk
¼ cup low-fat buttermilk
1⅓ cups all-purpose flour
1½ tsp. baking soda
1½ tsp. baking powder
  Black and fresh white
  pepper to taste
  Kosher salt to taste
⅔ cup corn kernels,
  blanched, chilled
⅔ cup russet potatoes,
  peeled, diced small
4 Tbsps. chives, minced
  Crème fraîche, low-fat,
  optional
  Salmon caviar, optional

R inse shellfish and set aside. Squeeze the crab meat to remove excess moisture.

Over low heat, sauté the onions and garlic in olive oil.

In a small mixing bowl, combine the eggs, milk and buttermilk. Set aside.

In a separate mixing bowl, sift in the flour, baking soda and baking powder, black and white pepper and salt into a large bowl.

Combine the wet ingredients to the dry ingredients and mix well. Add the corn, potatoes and chives. Add the seafood and mix well.

Drop 2 Tbsps. batter into a lightly oiled, hot cast iron skillet and fry until golden brown on both sides.

Serve with a dollop of crème fraîche and salmon caviar.

Charles Saunders
Eastside Oyster Bar & Grill
Sonoma, California

☆

Spiced Mahi Mahi
with Sweet Pepper Gazpacho Sauce

Clean the fish, then set aside.

Prepare a spice blend by grinding the fennel seed, peppercorns, cumin, garlic, chili powder and salt in spice mill on a coarse setting, or pulse in a coffee grinder until roughly chopped.

Thoroughly coat each filet with the spice blend and roast in a very hot pan to sear in the juices, or charbroil until the fish is translucent in the center. Serve the fish on top of the warmed Gazpacho Sauce.

Serves 4
Preparation Time:
  15 Minutes

Per Serving:
  189 calories,
  40 g protein,
  1 g carbohydrates,
  1 g fat

- 4 filets, 6 oz. each of mahi mahi, swordfish or scallops
- 2 Tbsps. fennel seed
- 1 Tbsp. black peppercorns
- 1 Tbsp. white peppercorns
- 1 tsp. Szechwan peppercorns
- 1 Tbsp. ground cumin
- 5 cloves garlic
- 1 Tbsp. hot chili powder
- ½ Tbsp. salt
  Sweet pepper gazpacho, recipe follows

Kevin Taylor
Zenith American Grill
Denver, Colorado

★

Sweet Pepper Gazpacho Sauce

Serves 4
Preparation Time:
20 Minutes

Per Serving:
101 calories,
4 g protein,
23 g carbohydrates,
1 g fat

1 qt. ripe tomatoes, diced
2 sweet red peppers,
   roasted, peeled (canned
   pimientos may be
   substituted)
2 garlic cloves
½ red onion
1 cucumber, peeled,
   seeded, diced
1 poblano pepper,
   chopped fine
2 serrano peppers,
   chopped fine
½ yellow or green bell
   pepper, diced
1 bunch green onions,
   chopped fine
1 tsp. cumin
2 Tbsps. balsamic vinegar
1 Tbsp. lime juice
   Salt to taste

 n a saucepan combine the tomatoes, peppers, garlic and onion. Bring the vegetable mixture to a boil, remove from heat and purée in a blender. Strain, set aside.

In a serving bowl combine the cucumber, poblano, serrano and bell peppers and green onions. Pour the hot tomato mixture over the vegetables. Season to taste with the cumin, vinegar, lime juice and salt.

Serve the sweet pepper gazpacho topped with the spiced mahi mahi.

Kevin Taylor
Zenith American Grill
Denver, Colorado

★

Tuna Steak with Wild Spring Vegetables

Season tuna with the pepper mix (recipe follows) and salt.

Heat a large sauté pan over medium high heat. Add 1 tsp. olive oil and sear tuna steaks. For a rare steak cook it 2 to 3 minutes on each side, depending on its thickness.

You can test the doneness by inserting the tip of a paring knife into the thickest part of the tuna. Remove it and quickly feel the temperature of the blade. If it is still cool, the tuna is very rare; if warm, the tuna is medium-rare; if hot, medium; if the blade is very hot, the tuna is well-done.

Remove the tuna steaks to a serving platter, cover with aluminum foil and allow to rest in a warm place.

In a sauté pan heat 1 tsp. olive oil and the new potatoes until potatoes begin to brown. Turn and add the garlic and mushrooms. Sauté until heated through. Remove from heat.

Slice tuna with a serrated knife and fan out on plates. Accompany with the vegetables. Garnish with herbs, a squeeze of fresh lemon and a sprinkle of sea salt.

Serves 4
Preparation Time:
  45 Minutes

Per Serving:
289 calories,
42 g protein,
16 g carbohydrates,
5 g fat

4 tuna steaks, 6 to 7 oz. each
4 tsps. mixed pepper blend (recipe follows)
1 tsp. sea salt or Kosher salt
2 tsps. olive oil
8 new potatoes, cooked tender, halved
1 clove garlic, minced
1 cup sautéed wild mushrooms
1 tsp. olive oil
1 lemon
  Chervil or opal basil as garnish

Daniel Orr
La Grenouille
New York, New York

⭐

Mixed Pepper Blend

Preparation Time:
  15 Minutes

- 3 Tbsps. coriander
- 1 Tbsp. fennel, minced
- 1 tsp. white pepper
- 1 tsp. black pepper
- 1 tsp. crushed red pepper
- 2 tsps. Chinese five-spice powder

 Place all ingredients in a spice grinder and grind to a coarse mix. This may also be done by cracking the peppers and spices with a rolling pin or with the bottom of a sauté pan.

Daniel Orr
La Grenouille
New York, New York

★

Wok-Charred Lobster with Oranges, Basil and Spicy Chiles

I n a large stock pot over a high heat, bring water to a rolling boil. Add the live lobsters and cook for 6 minutes. Remove lobsters from the water and shock in ice water. Remove the arms, claws and tail from the lobster. Carefully remove the claw and arm meat, trying to keep the meat whole. Split the lobster tail in half lengthwise. Remove the meat from the shell and remove the intestinal tracts.

In a large wok or skillet, heat the vegetable oil on high until it smokes. Add the lobster meat quickly, charring the outside of the meat for one minute. Remove the lobster, reduce heat and carefully add the Cointreau, stepping back as you place the wok back on the heat. When the Cointreau has evaporated, add the orange juice, soy and chile paste. Reduce by half. Add the bok choy, Thai basil and the lobster into the wok. Add the optional butter at this time, if using. Cook 2 to 3 more minutes or until the bok choy is wilted and the sauce is a light syrup consistency.

Serve immediately over hot boiled jasmine rice.

Serves 4
Preparation time:
  45 Minutes

Per Serving:
  598 calories,
  46 g protein,
  69 g carbohydrates,
  10 g fat

2 **Maine Lobsters, 1½ lbs. each**
2 **gallons water**
1 **Tbsp. vegetable oil**
4 **Tbsps. Cointreau liqueur**
1½ **cups orange juice**
2 **Tbsps. soy sauce**
1 **tsp. red chile paste**
2 **baby bok choy, cored, stalks separated**
4 **Tbsps. Thai basil or regular green basil, whole leaves**
2 **Tbsps. butter, optional**
1½ **cups Jasmine rice, cooked**

Peter McCarthy
Seasons
The Bostonian Hotel
Boston, Massachusetts

☆

131

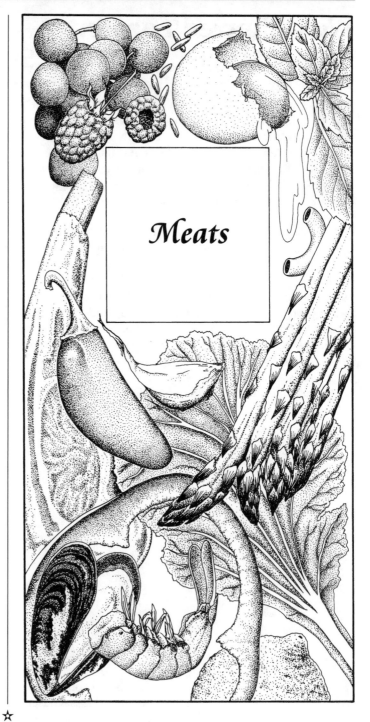

Meats

Roasted Beef Tenderloin with Chanterelles and Braised Leeks

T rim the tenderloin of all silverskin (outer white membrane). Marinate the meat in the garlic, thyme and ½ cup olive oil overnight in the refrigerator.

Cut chanterelles in large chunks to maintain the natural shape of the mushroom. Sauté over high heat in 2 Tbsps. olive oil until the liquid is cooked out and the mushrooms are becoming caramelized. At that point, add the chopped garlic and salt and pepper to taste, being careful not to burn the garlic. Reserve and set aside.

Cut the leeks, crosswise, just below the green leaves. Take the white of the leek and slice lengthwise in half. Wash in cold water, cut crosswise into ¼-inch half rings. Place in a pan with the chicken stock, salt and pepper and cook over medium heat until the liquid is gone and the leeks are soft. You may add 1 Tbsp. butter, if desired. Set aside.

Remove the beef from the marinade and season well with salt and pepper. Heat 2 Tbsps. olive oil in a sauté pan and sear the beef until it is golden brown on all sides. Remove from the pan and roast in a 350° oven for 15–20 minutes. Let rest in a warm place for 10 minutes before serving.

As the meat is resting, reheat the leeks and mushrooms.

A nice variation is to add a little veal stock to the mushrooms for a sauce or make a ragout of mushrooms and leeks when rewarming. You may also choose to grill the meat instead of roasting.

Serves 4
Preparation Time:
  45 Minutes (note
  marinating time)
Pre-heat oven to 350°

Per Serving:
  969 calories,
  73 g protein,
  26 g carbohydrates,
  64 g fat

2 lbs. beef tenderloin
4 large garlic cloves,
   peeled, crushed
1 bunch thyme
¾ cup olive oil
3 lbs. chanterelles
3 garlic cloves, chopped
   Salt and pepper to taste
2 large leeks
1 cup chicken stock

Cal Stamenov
Highlands Inn, Pacific's Edge
Carmel, California

Grilled Veal Scaloppine with Port Wine Reduction

Serves 4
Preparation Time:
  30 Minutes

Per Serving:
  519 calories,
  2 g protein,
  55 g carbohydrates,
  4 g fat

8 scaloppine of veal,
   ¼ lb. each
4 cups port wine
½ cup sugar
½ cup sherry wine vinegar
1 Tbsp. olive oil
   Salt and pepper to taste

n a saucepan over medium heat combine the port, sugar and vinegar. Reduce by ¾ or until the liquid becomes thick.

Rub your veal scaloppines with olive oil and sprinkle with salt and pepper. Grill over a hot fire to medium rare so that they stay tender.

Serve hot with the port wine reduction.

John Halligan
Halcyon
RIHGA Royal Hotel
New York, New York

Lamb with Mint and Vinegar

Make a well-flavored stock by cooking together the lamb shanks, garlic, white wine, veal stock and mint. Cook for 1 to 1½ hours. Strain, pressing well on the solids to extract all the flavor. Add a pinch of sugar.

Heat a heavy cast-iron pan, or a solid sauté pan. Season the lamb chops well with salt and coarse black pepper. Add oil to pan, then lamb chops, sear well, leaving them rare, 4 to 5 minutes per side. Remove and keep warm. Pour fat out of pan. Add the vinegar and reduce by two thirds.

Add stock and reduce rapidly by half. Swirl in butter. Add fresh chopped mint. Taste and adjust seasonings with salt, pepper and vinegar.

Serves 4
Preparation Time:
  2 Hours

Per Serving:
  550 calories,
  53 g protein,
  8 g carbohydrates,
  24 g fat

2 lamb shanks
4 heads of garlic, unpeeled, sliced in half across the cloves
2 cups white wine
1 qt. veal stock
1 bunch mint, coarsely chopped
Pinch of sugar
8 double rib lamb chops or loin of lamb chops (1½-inch thick)
Salt & coarse black pepper
1 Tbsp. olive oil
3 Tbsps. red wine vinegar
3 Tbsps. butter
Mint, chopped as garnish

David Waltuck
Chanterelle
New York City, New York

☆

Marinated Lamb Sandwich

Serves 6
Preparation Time:
   15 Minutes (note
   refrigeration time)
Cooking Time: 25 Minutes

Per Serving:
   705 calories,
   118 g protein,
   14 g carbohydrates,
   35 g fat

1 **leg of lamb, 6 lbs.,**
   butterflied
6 **slices of bread, ¾-inch**
   thick

Lamb marinade:
½ **tsp. paprika**
4 **Tbsps. cumin**
4 **Tbsps. fresh rosemary**
1 **tsp. cayenne pepper**
2 **Tbsps. turmeric**
½ **tsp. cinnamon**
¼ **tsp. nutmeg**
8 **garlic cloves**
½ **cup olive oil**

F or the marinade: Combine all the marinade ingredients except the olive oil in a food processor. Pulse a few times to roughly chop the herbs. Add the olive oil and purée.

Trim any excess fat from the leg of lamb. Cover the entire leg with the marinade, reserving ½ cup. Place lamb in a shallow dish, cover and refrigerate at least 3 hours or up to 48 hours.

Grill lamb 12 to 15 minutes on each side. Remove from heat and let stand 5 to 10 minutes.

Toast bread on the grill until brown, 2 to 3 minutes each side.

Slice lamb thinly and pile slices on top of each piece of toast. Drizzle with 2 Tbsps. marinade.

TRADE SECRET: Save remaining marinade for other uses: see Spicy Aioli and Roasted Red Pepper Salad, following pages.

Todd English
Olives
Charlestown, Massachusetts

Spicy Aioli

Place the red peppers on a grill or under a broiler until skins are blackened. Remove the skins and seeds.

Place the garlic, marinade and lemon juice in a food processor and purée. Add the red peppers and egg yolks and purée. While the machine is running, add the olive oil in a thin stream. Process until the mixture is thick and creamy. Add water to thin if necessary. Salt and pepper to taste.

Serves 6
Preparation Time:
  15 Minutes

Per Serving:
  348 calories,
  1 g protein,
  2 g carbohydrates,
  37 g fat

3 red bell peppers
1 large garlic clove, peeled
4 Tbsps. lamb marinade
    (see prior page recipe)
4 tsps. lemon juice
2 egg yolks
1 cup olive oil
5 Tbsps. water
    Salt and pepper to taste

Todd English
Olives
Charlestown, Massachusetts

☆

Roast Rack of Lamb

Serves 4
Preparation Time:
  30 Minutes (note
  marinating time)

Per Serving:
  853 calories,
  36 g protein,
  1 g carbohydrates,
  77 g fat

2 racks of lamb
½ cup olive oil
4 large cloves garlic,
  crushed
1 bunch rosemary
  Salt and pepper to taste

T rim lamb of excess fat or ask the butcher to do it. Combine the olive oil, garlic, rosemary, salt and pepper in a small bowl, and mix well. Place the lamb in a nonreactive baking pan. Pour the mixture over the lamb, cover, and refrigerate overnight or longer, turning the lamb frequently.

Prepare the hot coals for grilling. Remove the lamb from the marinade and season well with salt and pepper. Place on a hot grill. When the lamb is well seared, move to a cooler part of the grill and cook slowly for approximately 15 minutes or to desired doneness.

The following recipe for stuffed tomatoes with potato risotto is a wonderful accompaniment to the rack of lamb.

Cal Stamenov
Highlands Inn, Pacific's Edge
Carmel, California

☆

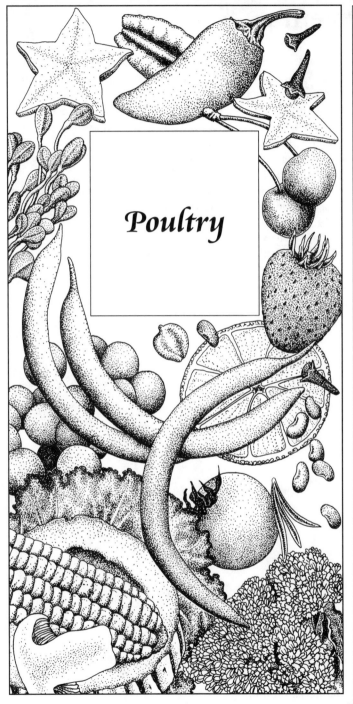

Poultry

☆

Chicken and Polenta

Serves 4
Preparation Time:
 45 Minutes

Per Serving:
 585 calories,
 59 g protein,
 47 g carbohydrates,
 14 g fat

8 **chicken breasts, 3 oz.**
 each
 Salt and pepper to taste
1 **Tbsp. garlic, minced**
1 **Tbsp. fresh rosemary,**
 chopped
4 **pieces of cold polenta,**
 3-inch squares
1 **Tbsp. olive oil**
1 **cup mushrooms, sliced**
¾ **cup shiitake**
 mushrooms, sliced
⅓ **each yellow, green and**
 red bell pepper, cut into
 strips
⅓ **cup sun-dried tomatoes,**
 soaked in warm water
½ **cup white wine**
1 **cup marinara sauce**
1 **Tbsp. olive oil**

Season the chicken breasts with salt, pepper, garlic and rosemary. Refrigerate until ready to grill or broil.
 Prepare the polenta according to package directions, finishing with the milk and Parmesan cheese option. Spread 1-inch thick in a cake pan and cook until firm. Cut in squares, then cut diagonally.

Chicken and polenta may be broiled, grilled or sautéed. (Broil for the lowest fat.)

While chicken and polenta are cooking, add the olive oil to a hot pan. Quickly sauté the vegetables, add the wine and reduce to half. Add the marinara sauce.

To serve, place chicken and polenta on individual serving plates, top with the vegetable tomato mixture.

Bill Cooper
Bella Saratoga
Saratoga, California

Chicken Couscous

Brush olive oil on chicken. Season and grill on both sides until cooked, approximately 3 minutes on each side. When cooked, remove from the grill and refrigerate. When cold, slice horizontally in 3 or 4 slices.

Place peppers, garlic cloves, cayenne, onion and chiles in blender and purée. Set aside.

Cook the instant couscous according to package directions. Season to taste with extra virgin olive oil and balsamic vinegar.

Add the pepper mixture to taste, then mix in the arugula and shiitake mushrooms.

Mold the couscous on the plate. Lightly brush the chicken slices with the remaining vinegar dressing and fan the chicken around the couscous.

Garnish with chopped chives, diced tomatoes and parsley sprigs

Serves 4
Preparation Time:
  45 Minutes

Per Serving:
  586 calories,
  42 g protein,
  75 g carbohydrates,
  11 g fat

  4 chicken breasts,
    skinless
  1 Tbsp. olive oil
  10 red bell peppers,
    roasted, peeled
  6 garlic cloves
  1 pinch cayenne
  ½ onion, minced
  1 pinch red dried chiles
  2 cups quick-cooking
    couscous
    Extra virgin olive oil, to
    taste
    Balsamic vinegar, to
    taste
  ¼ cup shiitake
    mushrooms, sautéed
  ¼ cup arugula
  2 Tbsps. chives, chopped
  1 tomato, skinned,
    seeded and diced
  4 sprigs parsley

Christopher Gross
Christopher's
Phoenix, Arizona
☆

141

Coriander Chicken

Serves 4
Preparation Time:
   30 Minutes (note
   marinating time)

Per Serving:
   382 calories,
   27 g protein,
   .5 g carbohydrates,
   30 g fat

4 **chicken breast halves,**
   halved, skin removed
½ **cup olive oil**
⅓ **cup fresh lemon juice**
   Salt and black pepper
   to taste
2 **garlic cloves, minced**
1 **cup coriander seeds,**
   toasted

R inse chicken and pat dry. Arrange chicken in a glass or enamel baking dish.
   In a small bowl, combine the olive oil, lemon juice, salt and pepper, and garlic. Mix well.
   Pour over chicken and turn pieces to coat evenly.
   Cover and refrigerate several hours or overnight, turning pieces occasionally.
   Before cooking, rub the chicken with the coriander seeds.
   Sear on high heat in an iron skillet on both sides and finish in an oven for 20 minutes or grill over hot coals.

Marion Gillcrist
The Double A
Santa Fe, New Mexico

☆

Cowboy Coffee-Rubbed Quail with Grits

Place quail in nonreactive bowl and toss with coffee, sage and garlic. Cover with plastic and reserve in refrigerator for 24 hours.

Combine water and salt in saucepan over medium heat; bring to a rolling boil. Whisk in grits; reduce heat. Simmer 15 minutes uncovered. Remove from direct heat; whisk in butter; reserve. Keep warm.

Heat olive oil in heavy skillet over medium heat. Sear quail on all sides. Transfer skillet to a 450° oven and roast quail 6 to 8 minutes.

Remove quail from oven and transfer to a platter; let rest 3 to 5 minutes.

To serve, spoon some grits in the center of each plate. Place 2 quails on top. Garnish with parsley sprigs and lemon wedges.

The mushroom ragout by Marion on page 177 is a wonderful accompaniment to this dish.

Serves 2
Preparation Time:
   30 Minutes (note
   refrigeration time)
Preheat oven to 450°

Per Serving:
   868 calories,
   53 g protein,
   94 g carbohydrates,
   53 g fat

4 whole quail, wingtips and legs trimmed
4 Tbsps. coffee, freshly ground
1 Tbsp. fresh sage, minced
2 tsps. fresh garlic, finely minced
4 cups water
1 tsp. salt
2 cups grits
4 Tbsps. unsalted butter, slightly chilled
   Olive oil
   Parsley for garnish
   Lemon wedges for garnish

Marion Gillcrist
The Double A
Santa Fe, New Mexico

Tarpy's Indiana Duck

Serves 8
Preparation Time:
  2 Hours
Pre-heat oven to 350°

Per Serving:
  784 calories,
  43 g protein,
  1 g carbohydrates,
  48 g fat

4 **fresh ducks**
  Kosher salt
  Black ground pepper
1 **bunch thyme, cleaned,**
  chopped
1 **Tbsp. vegetable oil**
1 **qt. rich chicken stock**
  Apricot mint glaze,
  recipe follows

With the duck sitting breast side up, pull the wings out and cut off the tips at the first joint. Remove the neck and gizzards from the bird's cavity and reserve. Cut along the Kiel bone, the bone that divides the breast into two sections. The idea is to remove the half-breast in one piece, skin on. With long strokes, follow the breast cavity until reaching the bottom of the breast; cut through the wing joint to disconnect from the carcass. Next, pop the leg joints out of their sockets and cut to remove the leg and thigh. By cutting under the thigh bone, remove and cut at the leg joint.

Season the ducks with salt, pepper and thyme.

In a large sauté pan, add oil until it is smoking hot. Sear the legs first, then the breasts. Place legs in a roasting pan, pour stock over, cover and cook in a 350° oven for 1 hour and 15 minutes, or until the meat is very tender. Remove from the oven. Finish the duck breast in the oven for about 30 minutes before the legs are finished.

Serve one half-breast with one leg as a portion with the apricot mint glaze.

Michael Kimmel
Tarpy's Roadhouse
Monterey, California

Apricot Mint Glaze

In a large pot heat all the ingredients, except the mint, slowly to a simmer.

Remove from heat and add the mint after mixture has cooled. Refrigerate.

Yield: 2¼ cups
Preparation Time:
  30 Minutes

Per Serving:
  194 calories,
  1 g protein,
  51 g carbohydrates

  2 cups apricot preserves
  ½ cup rice vinegar
  ¼ bunch mint, chopped
  ½ tsp. garlic, minced
  ½ tsp. shallots, minced
      Kosher salt and black
      pepper to taste
  ½ tsp. red chile flakes

Michael Kimmel
Tarpy's Roadhouse
Monterey, California

MooGoo Gaipan Stir-Fry

Serves 4
Preparation Time:
 45 Minutes

Per Serving:
 206 calories,
 21 g protein,
 20 g carbohydrates,
 4 g fat

1½ Tbsps. vegetable oil
 ½ lb. chicken breast meat, sliced
 ½ cup yellow onions, sliced
 ¼ cup canned water chestnuts, sliced
 ¼ cup canned bamboo shoots, sliced
 ¼ cup carrots, julienned
 1 cup fresh white button mushrooms
 1 cup fresh mushrooms, shiitake or chantrelles
 ½ cup snowpeas, with strings pulled off
 1 cup chicken broth
 ¼ tsp. salt
 ⅛ tsp. white pepper
 ⅔ tsp. sugar
 2 Tbsps. oyster sauce
 2 tsp. Kitchen Bouquet, optional
 2 Tbsps. cornstarch powder mixed with 2 Tbsps. water
 Garnish: fresh enoki mushrooms or green onion strips

Heat wok until hot and swirl vegetable oil. Add the chicken and sauté until browned.

Add sliced onions, water chestnuts, bamboo shoots, carrots mushrooms, and snowpeas and then continue to brown one more minute. Add chicken broth and cover with lid. Let simmer for 2 minutes covered.

Open lid and season with salt, pepper and oyster sauce. Add Kitchen Bouquet to color the sauce brown. Finally, thicken with cornstarch solution and garnish with enoki mushrooms or green onions on top.

Serve with steamed rice or over noodles.

David SooHoo
SooHoo's Market
Sacramento, California

☆

Roast Duck with a Curry of Honey, Cloves, Ginger and Hot Peppers

Remove the neck, gizzards, liver, etc. Trim off the feet and separate the ducks breast, and legs, leaving the meat on the bones.

Prepare a dry spice rub by combining the curry, cloves, jalapeños, salt and cumin seeds.

Sprinkle this mixture liberally over the ducks breasts and legs. Place on racks and let stand for 5 to 6 hours at room temperature.

Prepare a duck glaze by combining the honey, ginger, water and orange juice. Use a pastry brush to spread the glaze across the ducks.

Roast ducks in a 300° oven until breasts are medium-cooked, approximately 25 to 30 minutes, and legs are tender, approximately 1 hour.

Wonderful accompaniments to this dish are the Peach Chutney and the Saffron Rice Pilaf.

Serves 12
Preparation Time:
   45 Minutes (note
   marinating time)

Per Serving:
   551 calories,
   54 g protein,
   25 g carbohydrates,
   25 g fat

   6 **ducks, 4½ lbs. each,**
      fresh or frozen
   8 **Tbsps. curry powder**
   2 **tsps. cloves, ground**
   3 **jalapeños**
   ⅔ **cup Kosher salt**
   4 **Tbsps. cumin seed,**
      toasted, finely ground
   2 **Tbsps. orange zest,**
      finely chopped
   1 **cup honey**
   ½ **cup fresh ginger, peeled**
      and grated
   ½ **cup water**
   1 **cup orange juice**

Charles Saunders
Eastside Oyster Bar & Grill
Sonoma, California

☆

Barley-Quinoa with Clams and
Smoky Tomatoes

Calrose and Wild Rice Pilaf

Fettuccine with Tomatoes, Fennel,
Olives and Walnuts

Linguini di Capra

Paella a la Valenciana

Penne Pasta Tossed with Grilled
Tomato Sauce

Risotto ala Zucca

Risotto Verde

Risotto with Tomatoes, Swiss Chard
and Pancetta

Risotto with Wild Mushrooms and
Asparagus

Rock Shrimp and Fennel Linguini

Saffron Rice Pilaf

Sautéed Shrimp and Penne with
Rice Cream

Sticky Rice and Smoked Salmon
with a Red Miso Vinaigrette

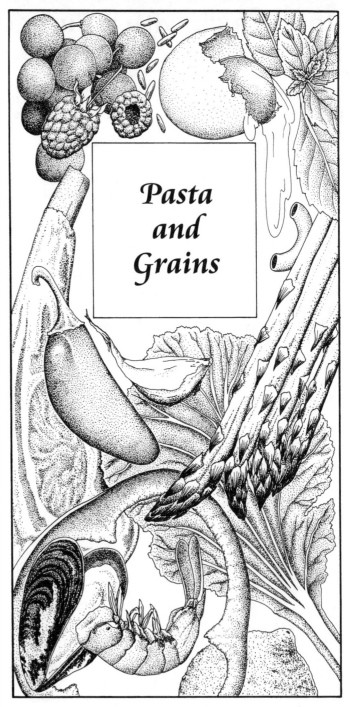

Pasta
and
Grains

Barley-Quinoa Risotto with Clams and Smoky Tomatoes

S moke tomatoes on a Weber grill, if possible. Otherwise, spread tea leaves in a foil-lined cast iron skillet. Place a steamer rack in skillet and arrange tomatoes on top. Cover loosely with foil and set over medium heat. Smoke 30 minutes, turning once. Set aside to cool, then peel and chop.

Melt butter in large, heavy-bottomed kettle over medium heat. Add the onions and pearl barley and sauté until golden. Add the stock or water, 1 lemon and the bay leaves. Bring to boil, then reduce heat and simmer, uncovered, stirring often, until barley is barely tender, about 30 minutes. Stir in the quinoa and cook, stirring often, until both grains are tender and most liquid is absorbed.

Meanwhile, heat olive oil in heavy skillet over high heat. Add garlic and sauté briefly, then remove with slotted spoon and discard. Stir in white wine, along with juice from the remaining halved lemon, smoky tomatoes and clam juice. Bring almost to a boil, then reduce heat, add the clams and simmer until all the clams open. Keep warm.

When the grains are cooked, remove and discard the lemon and bay leaves. Stir in chopped thyme and season liberally with salt and pepper.

Spoon into large serving bowls. Arrange 3 clams on one side of each serving and, using slotted spoon, ladle smoky tomatoes onto the other side.

Serves 6
Preparation Time:
  45 Minutes

Per Serving:
  495 calories,
  16 g protein,
  73 g carbohydrates,
  14 g fat

3 **large ripe tomatoes**
½ **cup black tea leaves**
3 **Tbsps. unsalted butter**
2 **onions, peeled, diced**
2 **cups pearl barley**
8 **cups defatted chicken stock, vegetable stock or water**
2 **lemons, halved**
3 **bay leaves**
¾ **cup quinoa, washed well**
2 **Tbsps. extra virgin olive oil**
2 **garlic cloves, peeled, crushed**
1 **cup dry white wine**
1 **cup clam juice**
1½ **dozen littleneck clams, well scrubbed**
¼ **cup chopped fresh thyme**
  Salt and freshly ground black pepper to taste

Paul O'Connell
Providence
Brookline, Massachusetts

★

Wild Rice Pilaf

Serves 4
Preparation Time:
45 Minutes

Per Serving:
360 calories,
8 g protein,
56 g carbohydrates,
11 g fat

1 Tbsp. butter
1 Tbsp. olive oil
½ medium onion, finely
    diced 1 medium-sized
    fennel bulb, quartered
    lengthwise, cored,
    finely diced
1 clove garlic, chopped
¼ cup white wine
    Salt and pepper
2 cups vegetable or
    chicken stock
1 cup Calrose rice, rinsed
    well and drained
    Zest of one lemon
½ cup cooked wild rice
2 Tbsps. pine nuts,
    toasted
2 Tbsps. chopped parsley

Heat butter and oil in a large skillet. Add onions and sauté 5 minutes or until tender. Add fennel, garlic, wine and salt and pepper to taste. Cook until pan is nearly dry.

Bring stock to a boil in a small saucepan. Meanwhile, add the Calrose rice to the skillet, and sauté for about 5 minutes, stirring as needed. Add the lemon zest, and pour in the boiling stock, stirring to moisten the rice.

Cover, lower the heat, and cook for about 7 to 10 minutes or until the rice is tender. Remove from heat and mix in the wild rice, pine nuts, and parsley into the Calrose mixture.

This dish makes a delicious accompaniment to roasted duck or chicken.

Chris Needham
Trio Bistro & Bar
Tucson, Arizon

★

Fettuccine with Tomatoes, Fennel, Olives and Walnuts

Toast walnuts on a sheet pan in a 350° oven for 6 minutes or until they become fragrant.

Toss tomatoes with the olives, garlic, 1 Tbsp. olive oil, salt and pepper. Let marinate under refrigeration for at least 1 hour.

Sauté the fennel in 1 Tbsp. oil for 20 seconds. Add the tomato mixture and sauté until the tomatoes just start to break down.

Deglaze with the white wine and season with salt and pepper.

Meanwhile, cook pasta in hot water, drain and toss in the pan. Transfer to a serving bowl, toss with tomato mixture, and garnish with the toasted walnuts and Parmesan.

Serves 4
Preparation Time:
  30 Minutes (note marinating time)

Per Serving:
  794 calories,
  23 g protein,
  85 g carbohydrates,
  43 g fat

1 cup walnut pieces
2 cups Roma tomatoes, chopped
2 cups yellow tomatoes, chopped
1 cup kalamata olives, pitted, cut in half lengthwise
2 garlic cloves, chopped
2 Tbsps. extra virgin olive oil
  Salt and pepper to taste
1 fennel bulb, quartered lengthwise, cored, thinly sliced
¼ cup white wine, or to taste
1 lb. fettuccine, cooked al dente
  Grated Parmesan cheese to taste

Chris Needham
Trio Bistro & Bar
Tucson, Arizona

Linguini di Capra

Serves 2
Preparation Time:
30 Minutes

Per Serving:
290 calories,
9 g protein,
52 g carbohydrates,
2 g fat

⅓ **cup green onions, sliced, including stems**
1 **Tbsp. garlic, chopped**
2 **Tbsps. olive oil**
1½ **cups vegetable stock**
¼ **cup white wine**
2 **Tbsps. sun-dried tomatoes rehydrated in warm water**
¾ **cup mushrooms, sliced**
1 **cup fresh tomatoes, diced**
4 **slices roasted eggplant, ½-inch each, julienned**
10 **fresh basil leaves, coarsely chopped**
½ **lb. fresh linguini, cooked al dente**
2 **Tbsps. parsley, chopped**
Goat cheese or Parmesan cheese to taste

Sauté the onion and garlic in oil quickly over high heat until tender. Reduce heat and add the vegetable stock and wine, cooking until the mixture is reduced by one-third. While the mixture is reducing, add the sun-dried tomatoes and mushrooms.

Then, add the fresh tomatoes, roasted eggplant and basil and heat until all the vegetables are hot. Toss in the cooked pasta, and continue to cook until the extra liquid is absorbed.

Serve on individual plates and garnish the top with parsley and goat or Parmesan cheese to taste.

Bill Cooper
Bella Saratoga
Saratoga, California

Paella a la Valenciana

Heat a paella pan or large stock pot with olive oil and sauté the chicken pieces and pork until brown on the outside. Remove from pan, set aside.

Add the onions, garlic cloves and the peppers to the pan and sauté until tender. Add the tomatoes and let them cook for 2 to 3 minutes. Return the chicken and pork to the pan.

Stir in the rice, squid and sea bass. Add the stock and bring the mixture to a simmer. Add the peas and beans.

Cook over low heat for 10 minutes, then add the saffron, parsley and remaining seafood.

Cook for another 8 minutes. Then remove from heat and let rest for 5 minutes.

Serve with lemon wedges around the paella pan.

Serves 6 to 8
Preparation Time: 1½ Hours

Per Serving:
  489 calories, 51 g protein,
  31 g carbohydrates, 16 g fat

¼ cup olive oil
1 lb. chicken, cut into 8 pieces
½ lb. pork loins, salted, peppered and diced
  Salt and pepper to taste
¼ onion, finely chopped
3 garlic cloves, chopped
½ red bell pepper, diced
½ green bell pepper, seeded, diced
¼ lb. tomato, skinned, chopped
1 lb. short grain rice
½ lb. squid, cleaned, with tentacles
½ lb. sea bass or grouper, diced small
2 cups chicken stock
2 cups clam juice or shellfish stock
⅓ cup sweet green peas
⅓ cup green beans, cut
  A few saffron threads
1 Tbsp. parsley, chopped
6 large whole prawns
12 large Manila clams
12 mussels
¼ lb. scallops
½ lb. shelled small to medium raw shrimps
  Lemon wedges for garnish

Lucas Gasco
Zarzuela
San Francisco, California

☆

Penne Pasta Tossed with Grilled Tomato Sauce

Serves 4
Preparation Time:
  30 Minutes

Per Serving:
  257 calories,
  10 g protein,
  38 g carbohydrates,
  7 g fat

8 **Roma tomatoes, grilled**
  or roasted
1 **red onion wedge, grilled**
2 **tsps. olive oil**
2 **Tbsps. garlic, chopped**
  Hot pepper flakes to
  taste
  Salt and pepper to taste
1 **tsp. red wine vinegar**
2 **Tbsps. chopped basil**
3 **Tbsps. Italian parsley**
1 **lb. penne pasta, cooked**

T oss Roma tomatoes and onion with olive oil and grill until dark. Chop onions and tomatoes.

In a sauté pan, add the garlic, pepper flakes, chopped tomato and onion with salt and pepper to taste.

Add water if needed. Add vinegar, basil and Italian parsley.

Toss cooked pasta into sauce.

Marion Gillcrist
The Double A
Santa Fe, New Mexico

✩

Risotto alla Zucca

Cut squash and yams in half lengthwise. Remove seeds from squash. Bake both on a sheet pan at 350°, cut sides down, for about 15 minutes. Turn over and spread lightly with butter. Bake until soft and lightly caramelized, about 10 minutes more.

With a spoon, scoop pulp from the squash and yams, leaving the skins.

In a heavy pan, heat the olive oil and 2 Tbsps. butter. Add the onions, shallots and garlic. Heat over medium-low heat until translucent. Do not caramelize. Add the rice. Stir until well coated and glistening. Add the white wine. Slowly add the stock, allowing the rice to absorb the liquid in between additions. Stir continuously. Do not allow the rice to settle and scorch. Add the squash and yam pulps to the rice.

Finish with nutmeg, salt and pepper, remaining butter and Parmesan cheese. Allow to cook slightly to absorb flavors before serving.

Serves 4
Preparation Time:
 40 Minutes

Per Serving:
 405 calories,
 7 g protein,
 52 g carbohydrates,
 14 g fat

1 small (½ lb.) butternut squash
2 medium (½ lb.) jewel yams
3 Tbsps. butter
1 Tbsp. olive oil
¼ cup white onion, minced
2 Tbsps. shallots, minced
1 tsp. garlic
1¾ cups Arborio rice
1 cup white wine
3½ cups vegetable stock, hot
¼ tsp. nutmeg
1½ tsps. salt
1½ tsps. white pepper
¼ cup Parmesan cheese, grated, optional

Suzette Gresham-Tognetti
Acquerello
San Francisco, California

☆

155

Risotto Verde

Serves 6
Preparation time:
  45 Minutes

Per Serving:
  258 calories,
  8 g protein,
  32 g carbohydrates,
  7 g fat

4 **cups chicken or**
   vegetable stock
½ **lb. asparagus**
¾ **cups fresh shelled peas**
1 **bunch spinach, washed**
¼ **cup pancetta, diced**
½ **medium onion, minced**
1 **Tbsp. extra virgin**
   olive oil
1 **cup risotto (Arborio**
   rice)
1 **cup white wine**
   White pepper, freshly
   ground, to taste
½ **cup Parmesan cheese,**
   optional
¼ **cup butter, unsalted,**
   optional

P lace chicken or vegetable stock on stove. Bring to a boil and turn down. Blanch asparagus, peas and then spinach in stock. Shock each vegetable separately with ice water to stop cooking process and preserve color. Drain well.

In food processor, whirl half of the asparagus with half of the peas and all of the spinach, adding up to ½ cup of blanching stock. Purée until smooth. Reserve vegetable purée. Strain remaining stock and set aside.

In a heavy-bottom pot, sauté the pancetta, adding the onions and olive oil for 3 to 4 minutes. Add the rice and stir around so grains are coated with oil. Add the white wine. As the rice begins to take up liquid, begin adding the stock in ¼ cup increments, stirring constantly.

After approximately 25 minutes add 2 cups of stock. Rice should begin to become al dente Add the vegetable purée, allowing the juice to cook in. The rice should still be firm, but tender. Add the remaining peas and asparagus. Adjust seasonings.

Remove pot from the heat. If desired, add the Parmesan cheese and butter. Stir quickly to incorporate all ingredients. Serve immediately.

Suzette Gresham-Tognetti
Acquerello
San Francisco, California

✩

Risotto with Tomatoes, Swiss Chard and Pancetta

I n a heavy saucepan, heat the oil and sauté the onion over low heat for about 8 minutes until onion is soft but not brown. Stir in the rice and cook for 2 minutes.

Add a ladle of chicken stock and stir constantly until the rice absorbs the stock. Add another ladle and continue stirring until it is absorbed. Add the herbs and continue stirring in the stock, one ladle at a time, until all has been used. Cook until the rice is creamy and tender. Stir in the cheese.

While rice is cooking, cook the pancetta or bacon until crisp, then drain on a paper towel.

Heat the butter, then add the Swiss chard. Salt and pepper to taste. Toss the chard in the butter until it is wilted.

Divide the risotto among 4 plates, garnish with the crumbled pancetta and top with the Swiss chard. Arrange the tomatoes around the edge. Serve immediately.

Serves 4
Preparation Time:
  20 Minutes

Per Serving:
  467 calories,
  25 g protein,
  49 g carbohydrates,
  18 g fat

2 Tbsps. olive oil
½ large onion, chopped
1 cup Arborio rice
4 cups chicken stock, heated to boiling
2 Tbsps. mixed herbs, chopped (tarragon, basil)
¼ cup grated Asiago cheese, or to taste
12 slices pancetta or bacon, optional
1 Tbsp. butter
2 heads Swiss chard, stems removed
   Salt and pepper to taste
2 tomatoes, cored, sliced
2 yellow tomatoes, cored, sliced

Clark Frasier
Mark Gaier
Arrows
Ogunquit, Maine
☆

Risotto with Wild Mushrooms and Asparagus

Serves 6
Preparation Time:
30 Minutes

Per Serving:
313 calories,
10 g protein,
39 g carbohydrates,
11 g fat

1 bunch asparagus,
   peeled
6 to 8 cups beef or veal
   stock
¼ cup (½ stick) butter
2 cups button
   mushrooms, thinly
   sliced
2 cups wild mushrooms,
   thinly sliced
1 large onion, finely
   chopped
2½ cups Arborio short-grain
   rice
1 cup dry white wine
½ cup Parmesan cheese,
   grated, optional
   Salt and pepper to taste
½ bunch Italian parsley,
   chopped

Boil 4 cups water and blanch asparagus until bright green.

Cut off the top 2-inch of each asparagus spear and set aside.

In a food processor, purée the remaining asparagus stems with 1 cup of stock.

In a large saucepan, melt half the butter over medium heat. Sauté the mushrooms and onions. Add rice and stir to coat. Deglaze with wine, then bring to a boil.

Add one cup of stock at a time, stirring until rice absorbs liquid. Continue adding the stock until the rice is cooked.

Stir in remaining butter and Parmesan. Season to taste and garnish with parsley.

Todd English
Olives
Charlestown, Massachusetts

☆

Rock Shrimp and Fennel Linguini

eat oil in a sauté pan and cook the fennel, onion, peppers, shallots and garlic until vegetables are just starting to turn translucent.

Add the rock shrimp and cook for approximately 30 seconds more.

Add the marinara sauce. Heat thoroughly. Add the white wine and simmer for 30 seconds more.

Toss with warm linguini. Season with salt and pepper.

Place in a pasta bowl and garnish the rim of the bowl with cumin and fennel seeds and chopped chives

Serves 4
Preparation Time:
  25 Minutes

Per Serving:
  421 calories,
  12 g protein,
  6 g carbohydrates,
  4 g fat

1 Tbsp. extra virgin olive oil
½ bulb fennel bulb, julienned
½ red onion, julienned
½ red bell pepper, julienned
½ green bell pepper, julienned
2 tsps. shallots, minced
2 tsps. garlic, minced
½ lb. rock shrimp
1 cup low-fat marinara sauce
2 Tbsps. white wine
1 lb. linguini, cooked
   Salt and pepper to taste
1 tsp. ground cumin and ground fennel seed, mixed
1 tsp. chives, chopped

Erik Huber
McCormick & Schmick's
The Fish House
Beverly Hills, California

⭐

Saffron Rice Pilaf

Serves 4
Preparation Time:
  40 Minutes
Pre-heat oven to 325°

Per Serving:
  269 calories,
  5 g protein,
  40 g carbohydrates,
  9 g fat

  2 Tbsps. olive oil
  ½ cup onion, peeled and
     finely diced
  1 cup rice
  1 pinch saffron threads or
     powder (placed in a
     cheesecloth and
     steeped in stock)
  2½ cups stock, light in
     color, strong in flavor
     Salt and fresh ground
     white pepper to taste
  2 Tbsps. red bell pepper,
     finely diced, garnish
  2 Tbsps. black sesame
     seeds, garnish

I n a heavy sauté pan, warm olive oil over moderate heat. Add the onions and sauté until clear. Add the rice and stir. Add the saffron and stock, adjusting the seasonings to taste.

Cover and place in 325° oven; bake for 30 minutes.

Before serving garnish with red peppers and black sesame seeds.

Charles Saunders
Eastside Oyster Bar & Grill
Sonoma, California

Sautéed Shrimp and Penne with Rice Cream

S eason shrimps with salt and pepper, then lightly dredge in flour. Sauté in olive oil until golden brown. Add the garlic and deglaze the pan with wine. Add the capers, tomatoes, garlic, parsley, pasta and rice cream. Continue to cook and stir sauce so the liquids incorporate. Season with salt and pepper.

Before serving, garnish with basil and Parmesan cheese.

Serves 4
Preparation Time:
  20 minutes

Per Serving:
  452 calories,
  19 g protein,
  83 g carbohydrates,
  2 g fat

- 24 pieces large shrimp, peeled and de-veined
- ½ cup flour
- 2 Tbsps. olive oil
- ½ tsp. garlic, minced
- ½ cup Chardonnay
- 2 Tbsps. capers
- 1 cup tomatoes, diced
- 2 garlic cloves, minced
- 1 Tbsp. Italian parsley, chopped
- 1 lb. penne pasta, cooked al dente
- 1 cup rice cream, recipe follows
  Salt and pepper, to taste
  Basil sprig for garnish
  Parmesan cheese, grated, optional

Alan Wong
Alan Wong's Restaurant
Honolulu, Hawaii

☆

Rice Cream

Yields: 4½ cups
Preparation Time:
 35 minutes

 ½ **cup white rice,**
  uncooked and washed
2½ **cups clam juice**
1¼ **cups water, chicken or**
  beef stock

R inse the rice, then combine in a sauce pot with clam juice and water or stock. Bring to a boil and cook over low heat stirring occasionally to avoid burning.

When rice is fully cooked, about 30 to 45 minutes, purée in a blender until the rice grains are fully puréed.

Alan Wong
Alan Wong's Restaurant
Honolulu, Hawaii

☆

Smoked Salmon with Sticky Rice and Red Miso Vinaigrette on Mizuna Greens

R inse sushi rice under cold water for 3 minutes. Place rice in a heavy-bottomed 2 qt. pot and cover with water. Bring to a boil over high heat, cover pot and turn heat to low. Cook for 15 minutes until rice is done.

In a separate small pan, heat the seasoned rice vinegar with the sugar until it is dissolved. Set aside.

When the rice is done cooking, add the rice vinegar and incorporate into the rice. Add the sesame seeds. Remove from the cooking pot and place in small molds to form desirable shapes.

Toss the Mizuna greens with the cucumber and red onions. Place the rice molds over the salad and top with smoked salmon. Drizzle the red miso vinaigrette over the top before serving.

Red Miso Vinaigrette

Place the orange juice in a non-reactive saucepan and bring to a boil. Reduce to ¾ cup and set aside to cool.

In a blender, combine the red miso, orange juice and rice wine vinegar and purée. Slowly add the olive oil, cilantro and scallions until mix is thoroughly incorporated.

Taste dressing and add lemon juice and black pepper to taste.

Serves 6
Preparation Time:
  45 Minutes

Per Serving:
  104 calories,
  5 g protein,
  19 g carbohydrates,
  1 g fat

  1 cup Sushi rice
1¼ cups water
  ½ cup rice wine vinegar
  4 Tbsps. sugar
  ⅛ cup black sesame seeds
  ½ lb. Mizuna greens
  1 cucumber, peeled, diced
  ½ red onion, julienned
  ¼ lb. smoked salmon

Red Miso Vinaigrette
  3 cups orange juice
  3 Tbsps. red miso
  ¼ cup rice wine vinegar
  ½ cup olive oil
  2 Tbsps. cilantro, minced
  2 Tbsps. scallions, minced
  2 tsps. lemon juice
    Pepper to taste

Paul O'Connell
Providence
Brookline, Massachusetts

☆

Main and Companion Dishes

Bean Ragout

Sauté the onions in oil until transparent over medium heat. Add the potatoes and cook for 3 to 4 minutes. Add the garlic, tomatoes and water. Cover and simmer over low heat until the potatoes are tender, adding more water if necessary. Transfer the ragout to a sheet pan to cool. Set aside.

Cook the beans until very tender but still bright green. Plunge in cold water and cut on the bias 1½-inch long.

In a serving bowl, combine the beans with the potato mixture. Season to taste and toss to combine.

Serve at room temperature sprinkled with crumbled feta.

Serves 8
Preparation Time:
   30 Minutes

Per Serving:
   238 calories,
   5 g protein,
   19 g carbohydrates,
   16 g fat

   ¼ **cup virgin olive oil**
   1 **onion, minced**
   1¼ **lbs. potatoes, cut into**
      ½-inch cubes
   1 **clove garlic, minced**
   ¾ **lbs. tomatoes, finely**
      chopped
   2 **cups water**
   ¾ **lb. green beans, washed**
   ¼ **lb. feta cheese**

Paul Sartory
The Culinary Institute of America at Greystone
St. Helena, California

Braised Mushrooms

Serves 4
Preparation time:
  45 Minutes

Per Serving:
  334 calories,
  3 g protein,
  23 g carbohydrates,
  27 g fat

½ **cup olive oil**
½ **large onion, minced**
5 **garlic cloves, peeled**
1 **lb. mushrooms, porcini**
  or shiitake, sliced
½ **cup dry white wine**
1 **cup chicken stock**
1 **cup tomato sauce, Pomi**
  or good-quality sauce,
  strained
½ **tsp. thyme, dry**
1 **Tbsp. fresh mint,**
  julienned
  Salt and pepper to taste

I n ¼ cup olive oil, lightly sauté the minced onions and the garlic cloves.

Add the remaining ¼ cup of oil, if desired, and the mushrooms and sauté further.

Add the white wine, chicken stock and tomato sauce. Add the thyme and mint.

Cook slowly for 20 to 25 minutes, covered. Season with salt and pepper to taste.

This dish is a beautiful vegetable or side dish, or it can be served as a sauce over pasta or polenta.

Suzette Gresham-Tognetti
Acquerello
San Francisco, California

Collard Greens

I n a sauté pan, add the olive oil and garlic and lightly brown for 15 to 30 seconds.

Add ½ cup of chicken stock and chopped collard greens. Cook for approximately 30 to 45 minutes, while adding additional chicken stock.

Add salt, pepper and apple cider vinegar to taste.

Serves 6
Preparation Time:
  15 Minutes

Per Serving: 51 calories,
  1 g protein,
  2 g carbohydrates,
  4 g fat

3 Tbsps. olive oil
½ tsp. garlic, chopped
2 cups chicken stock
6 cups collard greens
  (2 bunches), chopped
  Salt and pepper to taste
  Apple cider vinegar to
  taste

Marion Gillcrist
The Double A
Santa Fe, New Mexico

Eggplant Sandwiches with Tomato Relish

Serves 8
Preparation Time:
15 Minutes

Per Serving:
  205 calories,
  8 g protein,
  9 g carbohydrates,
  15 g fat

2 **to 3 Japanese eggplant,**
   2-inch diameter, cut
   into ½-inch thick
   rounds
   Kosher salt
4 **Tbsps. olive oil**
½ **lb. feta cheese,**
   crumbled
3 **eggs, beaten**
¾ **cup fresh white**
   breadcrumbs

Sprinkle eggplant rounds with salt, let drain for 30 minutes, and blot dry.

Fry in 2 Tbsps. hot oil to brown on both sides, drain.

Divide feta among the eggplant rounds, and sandwich, with another round.

Dip each eggplant round, in the egg wash, then breadcrumbs. Fry sandwich in remaining oil until eggplant coating is brown and cheese has melted. Serve hot with the following tomato relish recipe.

Paul Sartory
The Culinary Institute of America at Greystone
St. Helena, California

Tomato Relish

Heat oil in a saucepan over medium high heat. Add the chopped tomatoes and tomato paste and cook until the liquid is reduced and tomatoes begin to fry. Place the mixture in a chinoise to drain, saving liquid.

Use the reserved liquid to sauté the onions until transparent. Add the garlic, tomato mixture, and vinegar and cook gently for 2 to 3 minutes.

Adjust seasoning to taste and serve at room temperature with fried eggplant rounds and parsley sprigs.

Per Serving:
144 calories,
1 g protein,
5 g carbohydrates,
13 g fat

½ cup olive oil
6 large tomatoes, finely chopped
1 Tbsp. tomato paste
1 onion, minced
1 tsp. garlic, minced
1 tsp. red wine vinegar
Parsley sprigs

Paul Sartory
The Culinary Institute of America at Greystone
St. Helena, California

Enchiladas Verdes with Tomatillo Sauce

Yield: 12 Enchiladas
Serves 6
Preparation Time:
  1½ Hours
Pre-heat oven to 350°

Per Serving:
  250 calories,
  12 g protein,
  17 g carbohydrates,
  16 g fat

  1 **Tbsp. vegetable oil**
  ½ **medium-size red onion**
    Salt & cayenne pepper
  3 **ears of corn, shaved**
  2½ **tsp. cumin seeds,**
    toasted and ground
  5 **garlic cloves, finely**
    chopped
  3 **jalapeño or serrano**
    chiles, seeded, thinly
    sliced
  3 **medium-size zucchini,**
    diced,
  3 **Tbsps. chopped cilantro**
    Peanut or vegetable oil
    for frying
  12 **corn tortillas**
  2 **cups smoked cheddar**
    cheese, grated, optional
  4 **cups tomatillo sauce,**
    recipe follows

Heat the oil in a large skillet and add the onion, ¼ tsp. salt, and 3 pinches of cayenne. Sauté over medium heat until the onion is soft, about 5 to 7 minutes. Add the corn, ½ teaspoon salt, the cumin, garlic, and chiles. Sauté until the corn is just tender, about 5 minutes. Add the zucchini and cook for 4 to 5 minutes, until the zucchini is tender but not soft. Set aside 1 tablespoon of the cilantro for garnish and toss the rest into the cooked filing. Add salt and cayenne pepper to taste.

Fill a heavy-bottomed medium skillet with ¼ inch of oil; heat to just the smoking point—the tortilla should sizzle when it touches the hot oil. While the oil is heating, lay out paper toweling on a work surface. Using a pair of tongs, dip a tortilla into the oil just long enough to heat it through, 2 to 3 seconds. The tortilla should still be very soft. Lay it on the paper toweling to absorb the excess oil. Repeat with the rest of the tortillas.

Lay the tortillas out on a work surface. Set aside ½ cup of cheese to sprinkle on top. Place ⅓ cup vegetables in the center of each tortilla and sprinkle with 2 Tbsps. cheese. Roll the tortillas, making sure that the filling and cheese extends to the edges.

Ladle 2 cups of the sauce (recipe follows) into the bottom of a 9×13-inch baking dish and place the enchiladas in the dish. Ladle the remaining 2 cups of sauce over the enchiladas and bake at 350°, covered, for 20 to 25 minutes, until they're hot and the sauce is bubbling. Sprinkle with the reserved cilantro just before serving.

Annie Somerville
Greens
© Fields of Greens Cookbook
San Francisco, California

Tomatillo Sauce

Pour a little water into a medium-size saucepan; add the onion, ½ teaspoon salt, and a pinch of cayenne. Cover and cook the onion without stirring, over medium heat until soft, about 5 minutes.

Add the bell pepper, tomatillos, and chiles. Cover again and cook until the tomatillos are very soft and have released their juices, about 15 to 20 minutes. If the sauce is acidic, add a little sugar to balance the flavors.

Purée in a blender or food processor until the sauce is smooth; season with ¼ teaspoon salt and more chiles or cayenne to taste. Add the cilantro and crème fraîche, if you're using it, just before serving.

COOKING SECRET: To save a little time, soak the tomatillos in warm water for a few minutes before husking them. The warm water softens the husk and loosens it from the slightly sticky skin of the tomatillo.

Yields: 4 cups
Preparation Time:
   30 Minutes

Per Serving:
   100 calories,
   3 g protein,
   17 g carbohydrates,
   3 g fat

1 yellow onion, thinly
   sliced
   Salt & cayenne pepper
1 green bell pepper,
   coarsely chopped
2 lbs. fresh tomatillos,
   husked
2 jalapeño or serrano
   chiles, seeded, chopped
4 Tbsps. chopped cilantro
2 Tbsps. crème fraîche,
   optional

Annie Somerville
Greens
© Fields of Greens Cookbook
San Francisco, California

★

Garden Paella

Serves 4
Preparation Time:
   45 Minutes
Cooking Time: 30 Minutes

Per Serving:
   289 calories,
   5 g protein,
   36 g carbohydrates,
   14 g fat

¼ **cup olive oil**
1 **large onion, chopped**
1 **red pepper, chopped**
3 **garlic cloves, crushed**
½ **tsp. thyme**
¼ **tsp. oregano**
2 **bay leaves, whole**
   Salt and pepper to taste
1½ **cups short grain rice**
3½ **cups vegetable stock**
   Pinch of saffron strands
1 **zucchini, cut into**
   ¼**-inch slices**
1 **summer squash, cut**
   into ¼**-inch slices**
6 **broccoli florets**
4 **cherry tomatoes**
2 **artichoke hearts,**
   quartered
¼ **cup small green peas**
   for garnish

n a large pan, heat olive oil and sauté onion, red pepper and garlic. Add thyme, oregano, bay leaves, salt and pepper.

In a paella pan or similar pan, heat 1 Tbsp. oil. Brown rice until coated and opaque. Add mixture from the first pan. Mix well.

Add saffron to vegetable stock. Place in paella pan and bring to a boil. Lower heat. Arrange zucchini, summer squash, broccoli, tomatoes and artichoke hearts on top of rice. Cover and simmer for 20 minutes.

Uncover, add peas, and simmer for 5 more minutes. Let settle for a few minutes before serving.

TRADE SECRET: To best extract the flavor from saffron, wrap it in foil and keep it in a warm place to dry. Then mix with warm stock.

Mario Leon-Iriarte
Dali
Somerville, Massachusetts

Grilled Asparagus with a Fig Dressing

Prepare the fig dressing in a saucepan over a medium heat. Heat the oil. Add the onions and cook until translucent, about 3 minutes. Add the garlic and cook one minute more. Add the figs, water, vinegar, ⅓ cup olive oil, salt and pepper. Cook until the figs are soft, but not falling apart, about 4 minutes. Remove from the heat and add 1 Tbsp. parsley and the basil.

Pre-heat your grill to its highest setting. Remove the tough bottoms of the asparagus. Mix the asparagus, 1 Tbsp. olive oil, salt and pepper. Place the asparagus on the grill and lightly char it, turning spears frequently. Be careful not to overcook the asparagus. It should take no more than 2 minutes to grill the asparagus. Remove the asparagus from the grill and sprinkle the spears with Romano cheese if using, 1 Tbsp. parsley and crushed red pepper.

To serve, pool 4 Tbsps. of fig dressing on a plate and arrange the asparagus on top of it. Serve warm.

Serves 4
Preparation time:
  20 Minutes

Per Serving:
  157 calories,
  3 g protein,
  13 g carbohydrates,
  11 g fat

1 Tbsp. vegetable oil
1 onion, small, diced
2 garlic cloves, minced
6 black figs, de-stemmed, diced
⅓ cup water
2 Tbsps. red wine vinegar
⅓ cup + 1 Tbsp. extra virgin olive oil
1 tsp. Kosher salt
¼ tsp. fresh black pepper, ground
2 Tbsps. parsley, chopped
1 Tbsp. basil, chopped
2 lbs. asparagus
  Romano cheese, optional
½ tsp. crushed red pepper

Peter McCarthy
Seasons
The Bostonian Hotel
Boston, Massachusetts

★

Grilled Eggplant with Balsamic Vinegar

Serves 8
Preparation Time:
   10 Minutes

Per Serving:
   197 calories,
   12 g protein,
   19 g carbohydrates,
   8 g fat

3 **eggplants, peeled, sliced crosswise into ½-inch circles**
   Vegetable oil spray
6 **ripe Roma tomatoes, sliced**
   Kosher salt & black pepper to taste
1 **cup Asiago cheese, grated**
2 **Tbsps. basil, chiffonade**
½ **cup balsamic vinegar**

Spray both sides of the eggplant with the vegetable oil spray.
   Grill or broil until tender.

Arrange on an oven-proof serving platter so that the eggplant overlaps. Place the tomato slices around the outside, season with salt and pepper and grated Asiago cheese.

Heat under a broiler until very hot. Sprinkle with basil and drizzle with balsamic vinegar. Serve right away.

Michael Kimmel
Tarpy's Roadhouse
Monterey, California

Horseradish Mashed Potatoes

P lace the potatoes in a saucepan and cover with water. Boil over medium-high heat for 25 to 30 minutes, until the potatoes begin to fall apart. Drain.

Mash the potatoes with a hand mixer until smooth. Add the milk slowly and continue beating until the potatoes are fluffy.

Season to taste with salt, pepper and horseradish.

Serves 4
Preparation Time:
  45 Minutes
Per Serving:

97 calories,
4 g protein,
21 g carbohydrates,
1 g fat

4 **medium-sized russet baking potatoes, peeled, quartered**
⅔ **cup skim milk**
  Salt and pepper to taste
2 **Tbsps., or to taste, horseradish, freshly grated**

Marion Gillcrist
The Double A
Santa Fe, New Mexico

Lemon Yogurt Mashed Potatoes

Serves 4
Preparation Time:
  30 Minutes

Per Serving:
  203 calories,
  6 g protein,
  42 g carbohydrates,
  2 g fat

4 **lbs. potatoes, Idaho or russet, peeled, cut into 2-inch chunks**
1 **cup unflavored yogurt**
2 **tsps. sugar**
½ **cup lemon juice**
    Salt & pepper to taste
2 **tsps. olive oil, optional**

ook the potatoes in a large pot of water until tender about 20 to 25 minutes. Drain them well and place them in the bowl of an electric mixer.

Slowly add the yogurt, sugar and lemon juice and beat until smooth.

Add salt and pepper to taste, and olive oil if desired.

John Halligan
Halcyon
RIHGA Royal Hotel
New York, New York

☆

Mushroom Ragout

eat olive oil in a sauté pan over medium heat. Add the mushrooms and sear to a golden brown. Add the garlic and herbs and sauté 1 minute more. Add the chicken stock and reduce by half. Remove from heat and rapidly stir in butter.

Yield: 2 cups
Preparation Time:
15 Minutes

Per Serving:
288 calories,
2 g protein,
4 g carbohydrates,
30 g fat

- 1 Tbsp. olive oil
- ¼ cup cremini mushrooms, sliced
- ¼ cup portobello mushrooms, sliced
- ¼ cup shiitake mushrooms, sliced
- 1 Tbsp. garlic, finely minced
- 1 tsp. fresh sage, chopped
- 1 tsp. fresh thyme, chopped
- 1 tsp. fresh rosemary, chopped
- 1 to 2 cups brown chicken stock
- 4 Tbsps. unsalted butter, slightly chilled, optional

Marion Gillcrist
The Double A
Santa Fe, New Mexico

★

Roasted Corn Succotash

Serves 6
Preparation Time:
  30 Minutes

Per Serving:
  150 calories,
  6 g protein,
  32 g carbohydrates,
  1g fat

6 ears roasted corn
½ lb. lima beans, cooked slightly, al dente
2 red bell peppers, diced
¼ bunch Italian parsley, roughly chopped
½ yellow onion, diced
½ lb. Blue Lake green beans, cut 1-inch long, blanched, shocked
1 carrot, diced
2 Tbsps. garlic, roasted, puréed
1 Tbsp. Kosher salt
1 tsp. black pepper, ground
1 cup rich chicken stock

Roast corn in 350° oven for 15 minutes. Cool.
In a large bowl, combine all the ingredients except the stock and mix well, At this point you can refrigerate the succotash until you are ready to use.

To serve, heat the succotash with the stock. Allow stock to reduce to a glaze. Season with salt and pepper.

Michael Kimmel
Tarpy's Roadhouse
Monterey, California

★

178

Spinach Cakes with Shiitake Mushrooms and Goat Cheese

Heat 1 Tbsp. olive oil in a large skillet and add the mushrooms, ¼ teaspoon salt, and a few pinches of pepper. Sauté over medium heat for 3 to 5 minutes. Add the garlic and scallions and cook for 1 to 2 minutes more. Transfer the mushrooms to a bowl.

Wilt the spinach over medium heat with the remaining tablespoon olive oil, ⅛ tsp. salt, and a few pinches of pepper. Allow the spinach to cool, then squeeze out the excess liquid in small handfuls and coarsely chop. Toss the spinach with the mushrooms.

Beat the egg whites to stiff peaks. In a medium-size bowl, combine the egg yolks, ricotta, and milk. Stir in the flour, baking powder, ¼ teaspoon salt, and a pinch of pepper. Stir the vegetables and goat cheese into the mixture; fold in the egg whites.

Spoon the batter into a lightly oiled skillet or griddle over medium-high heat, making 3-inch cakes. Cook each side for about 3 minutes, until browned, turning the cakes only once. Do not flatten them with the spatula.

COOKING SECRET: These delectable cakes are a favorite winter dish. The tangy goat cheese works well with the flavors of the spinach, shiitake mushrooms, and fresh scallions. Be sure to use a light-tasting goat cheese such as Montrachet; a strong goaty flavor will overpower the cakes. Serve the cakes as an appetizer or make larger cakes and serve them as an entrée. Serve with room-temperature salsa.

Yields:
24 3-inch pancakes
Serves 6
Preparation Time:
45 Minutes

Per Serving:
181 calories,
10 g protein,
14 g carbohydrates,
9 g fat

- 2 Tbsps. light olive oil
- ½ lb. fresh shiitake mushrooms, stems removed, sliced ¼-inch thick
  Salt & pepper
- 3 garlic cloves, finely chopped
- 2 scallions, both white & green parts, thinly sliced
- 1 bunch spinach, stems removed
- 2 eggs, separated
- ½ lb. ricotta cheese
- ½ cup milk
- ½ cup unbleached white flour
- 1 tsp. baking powder
- 2 oz. mild goat cheese, crumbled
  Vegetable oil for frying
  Salsa of choice

Annie Somerville
Greens
© Fields of Greens Cookbook
San Francisco, California
☆

Tomatoes Stuffed with Potato Risotto

Serves 4
Preparation Time:
 1½ **Hours**

Per Serving:
 227 calories,
 13 g protein,
 24 g carbohydrates,
 9 g fat

6 **tomatoes**
2 **large potatoes**
1 **cup milk**
2 **garlic cloves, chopped**
1 **rosemary sprig,**
  chopped
1 **cup chicken stock**
⅓ **cup goat cheese**
⅓ **cup Parmesan cheese**
  Extra virgin olive oil,
  optional

lanch the tomatoes in salted boiling water for 30 seconds, just to remove the skins. Place in an ice water bath.

When tomatoes are cool, remove all outer skin and cut off ½-inch of the top, reserving the tops for later use. Remove the inside of the tomato to form a cup.

Peel and slice the potatoes in ¹⁄₁₆-inch cubes. Place in a small pan over low heat and cook with the milk, chopped garlic and chopped rosemary until thick. Add the chicken stock, goat cheese and Parmesan cheese. Stir over low heat for about 45 minutes or until the potatoes are al dente.

Stuff the tomatoes with the potato risotto mixture and cover with the tomato tops.

Heat the tomatoes in 500° oven until warmed. Drizzle with extra virgin olive oil before serving.

Cal Stamenov
Highlands Inn, Pacific's Edge
Carmel, California

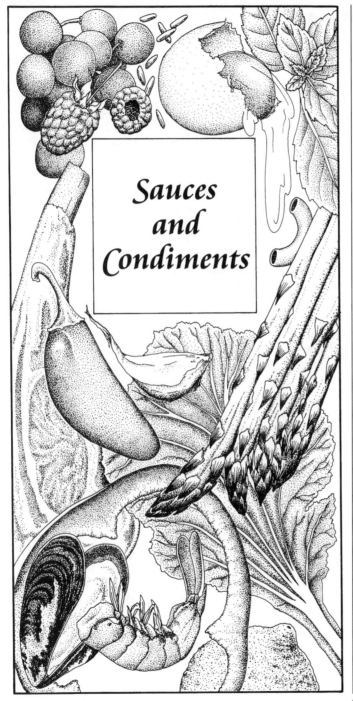

Sauces
and
Condiments

Artichoke Topping

Serves 6
Preparation time:
  30 Minutes

Per Serving:
  204 calories,
  1 g protein,
  2 g carbohydrates,
  18 g fat

36 whole, small, fresh
   artichokes
3 lemons, quartered,
   seeds removed
½ cup extra virgin olive oil
1 cup dry white wine
3 garlic cloves, sliced
   in half
   Kosher salt
   White ground pepper

Select small to medium artichokes. With a sharp knife, cut the stems off where they join the leaves. Slice the bottom horizontally, approximately ⅓ of the way up. Check to see if the thistle is apparent. Peel off the outer leaves until the artichoke is chartreuse in color. Cut in quarters. Place in acidulated water (approximately 2 lemons per gallon).

In a heavy-bottom pot place the olive oil, wine, garlic and artichokes. Squeeze the juice of 1 lemon over all and add to the pot. Lightly season with salt and pepper. Cover. Cook on low heat, checking every 5 to 7 minutes. After 15 minutes, if liquid has evaporated and chokes are not done, add ¾ to 1 cup water. Swirl around, making sure nothing is browning or sticking. Simmer until tender and virtually no liquid remains. Turn onto cookie sheet. Remove lemons. Spread to cool. Place in refrigerator.

After mixture has cooled, place contents in Cuisinart or blender. Pulse. Check salt and pepper. Add ¼ to ½ cup water to help smooth it out.

Hold here. Uses may vary. Use as filling, sauce, salad dressing, etc. Thin out as desired with oil, lemon, pasta cooking water, etc. Cook pasta and top with sauce.

COOKING SECRET: Try adding blanched peas or a chiffonade of mint.

Suzette Gresham-Tognetti
Acquerello
San Francisco, California

☆

Cucumber Compote

H alve the cucumbers lengthwise, then scoop out the seeds with a small spoon. Cut the cucumbers into cubes. Transfer them to a bowl and add the parsley, cilantro, onion, lemon juice, salt and pepper. Marinate 10 to 20 minutes before serving.

Serves 4
Preparation Time:
  15 Minutes

Per Serving:
  29 calories,
  1 g protein,
  6 g carbohydrates

  2 cucumbers, peeled
  ½ bunch Italian parsley,
     finely chopped
  ½ bunch fresh cilantro,
     finely chopped
  ½ red onion, coarsely
     chopped
     Juice of 1 lemon
     Salt and pepper to taste

Clark Frasier
Mark Gaier
Arrows
Ogunquit, Maine
✩

Lemon or Lime Barley Water

Serves 2
Preparation Time:
  10 Minutes

Per Serving:
  138 calories,
  2 g protein,
  33 g carbohydrates

  3 Tbsps. pearl barley
4½ cups water
  4 Tbsps. freshly squeezed
    lemon or lime juice
  3 Tbsps. honey or sugar,
    or to taste

Place water in a heavy pot with the barley and bring to a boil. Reduce the mixture by 50% over high heat. Strain the liquid into a clean glass container. Mix in the lemon or lime juice and honey or sugar, stirring well. Serve well chilled.

Kevin Graham
Graham's
River Ridge, Louisiana

☆

Peach Chutney

I n a large stock pot combine the lemon juice, sugar, water, duck glaze and spices, bringing the mixture to a boil. Reduce the heat, and simmer until the liquid is a maple syrup-like consistency.

In hot boiling water, blanch each fruit individually and drain. Set aside.

Combine the syrup with the fruit. Cover and allow to stand several hours prior to serving.

Yields: 1 Quart
Preparation Time:
One Hour

Per Serving:
  68 calories,
  1 g protein,
  17 g carbohydrates,
  2 g fat

  Juice of 1 lemon
1 cup sugar 1 cup water
⅓ cup duck glaze or beef stock
½ tsp. Chinese five spice
3 apricots, pitted and cut into 8 pieces
4 peaches, pitted and cut into 8 pieces
3 plums, pitted and cut into 6 pieces
4 nectarines, pitted and cut into 8 pieces

Charles Saunders
Eastside Oyster Bar & Grill
Sonoma, California
☆

Salsa Verde

Yield: 1 cup
Preparation time:
  15 Minutes

Per Serving:
  128 calories,
  1 g protein,
  1 g carbohydrates,
  14 g fat

½ cup extra virgin olive oil
1 scallion, white and
   green parts, coarsely
   chopped
1 small garlic clove,
   chopped
1 packed cup parsley
   sprigs
1 packed cup watercress
   sprigs
½ tsp. salt
2 to 3 pinches of pepper
½ Tbsp. fresh lemon juice
1 tsp. champagne vinegar
½ tsp. drained capers,
   rinsed

lace the olive oil in a blender; add the remaining ingredients and blend until smooth. Serve this sauce freshly made.

This is a smooth, piquant green sauce—delicious served in the winter with grilled vegetables or Spinach Cakes with Shiitake Mushrooms and Goat Cheese. In summer, include some basil along with the watercress and parsley.

Annie Somerville
Greens
© Fields of Greens Cookbook
San Francisco, California

☆

Tomato Ginger Coulis

I n a large stock pot heat the olive oil; add the ginger and garlic. When slightly browned, add the tomatoes and chicken stock.

Simmer over low heat for 45 minutes. Season with salt and pepper to taste.

Serves 4
Preparation Time:
  One Hour

Per Serving:
  102 calories,
  2 g protein,
  7 g carbohydrates,
  1 g fat

  2 Tbsps. olive oil
  1 piece of ginger, 3 inches long
  6 garlic cloves
1½ cups tomatoes, diced
  6 cups chicken or vegetable stock
     Salt and pepper to taste

Alan Wong
Alan Wong's Restaurant
Honolulu, Hawaii

☆

Almond Tuile Cookies with
Coconut Orange Sorbet,

Anise, Pear and Cranberry Cobbler
with Vinegar Dough

Caramelized Baby Eggplant

Cranberry and Orange Granita

Low-Fat Carrot Cake
with Sour Cherry Coulis

Oeufs à la Neige

Roasted Fruits with Cinnamon

Ruby Red Grapefruit Segments
with Vermouth Granita

Strawberries with
Balsamic Vinaigrette

Sweet Vanilla Polenta

Vanilla and Chocolate Angel Food
Cakes, Bananas, Strawberries

Warm Berry Sundae

Final
Temptations

Almond Tuile Cookies
with Coconut Orange Sorbet

C ream the butter and sugar together in a bowl with a wooden spoon. When soft and fluffy, add the egg whites, stirring only enough to blend. Add the flour and begin folding it in until almost blended. Add the crushed almonds, almond extract and salt.

Drop 4 Tbsps. of batter onto a greased sheet pan, allowing 3-inch of space between them. Dip a fork into water and flatten each to ⅛-inch thickness.

Bake at 350° for about 15 minutes or until just evenly brown. Immediately lift off the tray with a spatula and lay each cookie over upside down cups to form a bowl.

If the cookies harden before being removed from the sheet pan, return to the oven for 30 seconds to soften again.

Yields: 20 wafers
Preparation Time:
  30 Minutes
Pre-heat oven to 350°

Per Serving:
  88 calories,
  2 g protein,
  7 g carbohydrates,
  6 g fat

4 Tbsps. melted butter
½ cup sugar
4 egg whites
¼ cup flour
1½ cups sliced almonds, crushed, lightly toasted
¼ tsp. almond extract
  Pinch of salt, optional

Kevin Taylor
Zenith American Grill
Denver, Colorado

★

Coconut Orange Sorbet

**Yields: 1 gallon,
  serving 10 to 12
Preparation time:
  One Hour**

Per Serving:
  203 calories,
  1 g protein,
  51 g carbohydrates

2½ cups sugar
 7 cups water
 ¼ cup fresh ginger,
    roughly chopped
1¾ cup grated sweetened
    coconut
 4 cups fresh squeezed
    orange juice
 ¾ cup fresh squeezed lime
    juice

 n a saucepan, combine the sugar, 2½ cups water and ginger, bringing the mixture to a boil. Reduce heat and simmer slowly for 2 minutes.

Remove from heat and set aside for at least 30 minutes. Strain the mixture to yield about 2½ cups syrup.

In a separate saucepan combine the coconut and 4½ cups water in a pan. Bring to a boil, simmer slowly for 2 minutes, then set aside for at least 30 minutes. Strain to yield 3½ cups coconut juice.

Combine the syrup, coconut juice and remaining ingredients and place in an ice cream maker. Freeze according to the manufacturer's instructions.

Kevin Taylor
Zenith American Grill
Denver, Colorado

☆

Anise-Pear and Cranberry Cobbler with Vinegar Dough

Mix all ingredients together.

Sauté in a large, very hot cast iron skillet until pears are soft and syrupy. Pour into another 10-inch skillet (cast iron) lined with rolled vinegar dough (recipe follows). Dot top with 4 oz. more butter (optional). Fold more rolled dough over top until completely covering top of cobbler.

Bake at 350° for 1 hour. Put sheet pan underneath to catch pear drippings.

Vinegar Dough for Cobbler

Cut first three ingredients together with knife until well-blended.

Pour in both liquids and fold dough together just until it starts to stick together. Do not overmix. It should look very cracked and pasty. Knead into a ball and roll out on a floured board (be sure to flour top of dough as well). Roll to ¼-inch thickness and place in the bottom of 10-inch cast iron skillet sprayed with Pam first. Leave a little hanging over the edge to fold over pears. Roll out a little more dough to finish top layer of cobbler.

Marion Gillcrist
The Double A
Santa Fe, New Mexico

Serves 6
Preparation Time:
1½ Hours
Pre-heat oven to 350°

Per Serving:
331 calories,
2 g protein,
49 g carbohydrates,
16 g fat

6 red pears, peeled and sliced vertically
2 tsps. freshly crushed anise seed
1 cup sugar
1 tsp. cinnamon
1 cup dried cranberries
¼ tsp. nutmeg
8 oz. butter, cut into pieces, optional

Vinegar Dough for Cobbler

Per Serving:
797 calories,
10 g protein,
67 g carbohydrates,
54 g fat

4¼ cups flour
1¾ cup butter, cold and cut into dime-size pieces
1½ tsp. Kosher salt
4 Tbsps. ice water
4 Tbsps. apple cider vinegar
Pam vegetable spray

Caramelized Baby Eggplant

Serves 6
Preparation Time:
  35 Minutes (note
  refrigeration time)
Cooking Time: 10 Minutes

Per Serving:
  75 calories,
  1 g protein,
  10 g carbohydrates,
  3 g fat

2 lbs. Japanese eggplants,
  small
1 qt. water
¼ cup sugar
1 Tbsp. rum
1 Tbsp. vanilla extract
1 cinnamon stick
  Small pieces of lemon
  rind
¾ cup low-fat sour cream
  or yogurt
  Sprigs of fresh mint for
  garnish

T hinly slice eggplant lengthwise, leaving them attached at the tops, to be fanned out later.

Bring water to a boil. Add sugar, rum, vanilla, cinnamon and lemon. Boil until water becomes lightly syrupy.

Add eggplants and cook gently for about 10 minutes, until done but slightly firm.

Remove eggplants and continue boiling syrup until it becomes heavy. Remove from heat.

Return eggplants to syrup and cool in refrigerator.

Serve fanned out on a shallow plate with a dollop of sour cream or yogurt and a sprig of fresh mint.

TRADE SECRET: This sweet dish is a Basque dish with Moorish influence from Northern Spain.

Mario Leon-Iriarte
Dali
Somerville, Massachusetts

☆

Cranberry and Orange Granita

Whisk together juices. Add water and season to taste with brown sugar. Freeze overnight.
Scrape to make a shaved ice.

Serves 6 to 8
Preparation Time:
   10 Minutes (note refrigeration time)

Per Serving:
   98 calories,
   1 g protein,
   24 g carbohydrates

   2 cups cranberry juice
   2 cups orange juice
   2 Tbsps. lemon juice
      Water, to taste
      Brown sugar, to taste

Gale Gand
Brasserie T
Chicago, Illinois

⭐

Low-Fat Carrot Cake with Sour Cherry Coulis

Serves 16
Preparation Time:
   One Hour
Pre-heat oven to 375°

Per Serving:
   329 calories,
   5 g protein,
   77 g carbohydrates,
   2 g fat

1½ **cups pitted prunes**
 6 **Tbsps. water**
 4 **cups carrots, grated**
 2 **cups sugar**
 1 **can crushed pineapple,**
    8 oz. 4 large egg whites
 2 **tsps. vanilla**
 2 **cups flour**
 2 **tsps. baking soda**
 2 **tsps. cinnamon**
 ½ **tsp. salt**
 ¾ **cups coconut, shredded**
    or flaked
1½ **cups dried sour cherries**
1¼ **cups fresh apple juice**

Coat a 9×13-inch baking pan with non-stick cooking spray; set aside.

Make a prune purée by combining prunes and water in a food processor. Pulse until prunes are finely chopped. Set aside.

Combine carrots, sugar, pineapple, prune purée, egg whites and vanilla in a large bowl; stir to blend thoroughly. Add the flour, baking soda, cinnamon and salt and mix well. Gently stir in the coconut.

Spread batter in prepared pan and bake about 45 minutes, or until center of the cake springs back when lightly pressed.

To make the sour cherry coulis, combine the cherries and apple juice in a small pan. Bring to a boil. Remove from heat and cover. Allow mixture to steep 30 minutes. Put in blender and purée.

Cool in pan. Cut into 16 pieces. Serve cake with sour cherry coulis.

Bradley Ogden
The Lark Creek Inn
Larkspur, California

☆

Oeufs à la Neige

Whip the whites until soft peaks form. While the mixer is still whipping, add the sugar and vanilla to stiff peaks. Using a plain or star tip, pipe the meringues into egg shapes. With a spatula, carefully lift the meringues and place in simmering water. Cook for about 1 minute on each side. With a slotted spoon, lift out the meringues and place in a pan with a thin layer of skim milk on the bottom. Chill.

At Seasons, we use melon, mango and prickly pear sauces. The red, yellow and green, make an attractive presentation as well as an interesting flavor combination. Any desired fruits may be used. It's simply a matter of puréeing the fruit and adding the desired amount of sugar.

To assemble, pour each of your three sauces on a plate. Place an oeuf à la neige on each sauce. Arrange slices of fresh fruit on the plate and place a scoop of sorbet in the center.

Serves 8
Preparation time:
  30 Minutes

Per Serving:
  200 calories,
  5 g protein,
  38 g carbohydrates,
  3 g fat

7 **egg whites**
1 **cup sugar**
1 **tsp. vanilla**
2 **cups fresh fruit of**
   choice: melon, mango,
   raspberry, strawberry,
   etc., puréed
   Sorbet
   Fresh fruit as garnish

Billy Boudreau
Seasons
The Bostonian Hotel
Boston, Massachusetts

☆

Roasted Fruits with Cinnamon

Serves 4
Preparation Time:
  45 Minutes
Pre-heat oven to 400°

Per Serving:
  370 calories,
  10 g protein,
  42 g carbohydrates,
  19 g fat

2 plums, quartered
2 peaches, quartered
2 pears, quartered
2 Tbsps. honey
2 Tbsps. brown sugar
2 Tbsps. red wine
½ tsp. cinnamon
⅓ lb. sliced almonds
¼ cup sugar
2 egg whites

Cut fruit in quarters and remove stones and seeds. Stir together honey, brown sugar, red wine and cinnamon, and toss with fruit.

Place in a baking dish and roast in a 400° oven until tender, about 20 to 30 minutes.

Toss almonds and sugar. Stir in egg whites until well mixed. Bake on a lightly greased sheet pan at 300°, turning with a spatula until golden brown and caramelized. Break up slightly and garnish fruit.

Gale Gand
Brasserie T
Chicago, Illinois

★

Ruby Red Grapefruit Segments with Vermouth Granita

Cut the grapefruits in segments or filets by removing the top and bottom of the fruit with a sharp knife, then cutting off the rind just enough to expose fruit. Then cut the tender filets from between the fibrous tissue. When all the segments are removed, squeeze the remaining grapefruit over the segments and toss with the honey. Reserve in the refrigerator.

Combine vermouth, water and sugar in a heavy-bottomed saucepan and bring to a boil. Remove from heat and stir until sugar has completely dissolved. Add the lemon and lime juice and zest, pour into a rectanglar baking dish, and allow to cool to room temperature.

Place level in a freezer and allow to freeze. For best texture, stir several times as it freezes. This gives a flaky texture. When solid, rake with a fork to produce a light, crystally ice.

Arrange the grapefruit segments on chilled plates in a flower design, each segment being a petal. Scoop out a portion of the granita and decorate with mint sprigs. Finally, spoon a little of the juice from the grapefruits over the segments and serve quickly.

COOKING SECRET: A few chopped mint leaves may be tossed with the grapefruit and honey if you want to increase the fresh, minty flavor.

Serves 6
Preparation Time:
   25 Minutes (note refrigeration time)

Per Serving:
   408 calories,
   1 g protein,
   75 g carbohydrates

   4 **red grapefruits**
   ½ **cup honey**
   6 **sprigs mint, optional**
   3 **cups vermouth**
   2 **cups water**
   1 **cup sugar**
      Juice of 1 lemon and grated zest
      Juice of 1 lime and grated zest

Daniel Orr
La Grenouille
New York, New York

★

Strawberries with Balsamic Vinegar and Red Wine

Serves 4
Preparation Time:
  15 Minutes (note refrigeration time)

Per Serving:
  53 calories,
  1 g protein,
  12 g carbohydrates

  1 basket (pint)
    strawberries
  1 to 2 Tbsps. sugar
  1 Tbsp. red wine, optional
1½ tsps. balsamic vinegar
  ½ tsp. lemon juice

R inse the strawberries and remove the stems. Cut the berries in half if they are large. Sprinkle sugar over the berries, toss and put in the refrigerator for 1 hour.

In a small bowl, combine the wine, balsamic vinegar and lemon juice. Pour over the berries and mix well before serving.

Suzette Gresham-Tognetti
Acquerello
San Francisco, California

Sweet Vanilla Polenta

W hen cooking polenta, make sure that the pan has a very thick bottom and that you stir the cornmeal mixture constantly with a wooden spoon.

Combine the milk, salt and vanilla bean halves (if using) in a large, heavy saucepan. Bring the mixture to a boil over high heat, then reduce to a simmer. Slowly add the cornmeal, stirring constantly, and cook, continuing to stir for 5 to 7 minutes. Remove the pan from the heat, stir in the sugar and vanilla extract (if using), and allow the polenta to sit covered for 5 minutes. Remove the vanilla bean halves, if necessary.

Divide the polenta among 6 to 8 dessert dishes. If desired, spoon a large dollop of mascarpone cheese or strawberry or apricot preserves in the center of each serving.

Serves 6 to 8
Preparation Time:
30 Minutes

Per Serving:
171 calories,
6 g protein,
30 g carbohydrates,
3 g fat

4 cups skim milk
 Pinch of salt
1 vanilla bean, split lengthwise, or 1 tsp. pure vanilla extract
1 cup finely ground cornmeal
½ cup sugar
¼ cup mascarpone cheese or strawberry or apricot preserves, optional

Kevin Graham
Graham's
River Ridge, Louisiana

☆

Vanilla & Chocolate Angel Food Cakes with Bananas and Strawberries

Serves 12
Preparation time:
  45 Minutes
Pre-heat oven to 350°

Per Serving:
  180 calories,
  6 g protein,
  39 g carbohydrates

  2 **cups egg whites**
  ½ **tsp. salt**
  ¼ **tsp. cream of tartar**
  1 **cup sugar**
  2 **tsps. vanilla**
  ½ **tsp. almond extract**
  1 **cup powered sugar**
  5 **oz. cake flour**
  2 **Tbsps. cocoa powder**
  3 **bananas**
     Brown sugar to taste
  1 **Tbsp. lemon juice**
  1 **pint strawberries**

Prepare the two angel food cakes separately. Whip 1 cup egg whites to soft peaks. Add ¼ tsp. salt and ⅛ tsp. cream of tartar. Slowly add ½ cup sugar to stiff peaks. Add the vanilla and almond extracts. Combine ½ cup powdered sugar with 3 oz. cake flour. Sift flour mixture over the egg whites. Quickly fold. Set aside.

To make the chocolate angel food cake, whip 1 cup egg whites to soft peaks. Add ¼ tsp. salt and ⅛ tsp. cream of tartar. Slowly add ½ cup sugar to stiff peaks. Combine the cocoa powder, ½ cup powdered sugar and 2 oz. cake flour. Sift flour mixture over the egg whites. Quickly fold.

You can use a piping bag to pipe into individual molds or into an 8-inch one. Do not grease the mold.

Place in a 350° oven for 15 minutes for individuals or about 30 minutes for a large. Cool upside down in the pan. Loosen the cake from the sides of the pan with a knife. You will have 6 of each cakes, or enough for twelve desserts. You can wrap the extras tightly in plastic.

Make a banana purée by blending 3 fresh bananas with brown sugar to taste, along with the lemon juice.

Make a strawberry purée by puréeing strawberries with sugar to taste. Pass through a fine sieve if desired.

To serve, slice angel food cakes in half and arrange with fresh fruit purée.

Billy Boudreau
Seasons
The Bostonian Hotel
Boston, Massachusetts

☆

Warm Berry Sundae

I n a blender, blend one basket of raspberries to purée for a sauce

To a warm skillet, add the Triple Sec and ¾ cup of the raspberry purée. Heat until warm, then add the remaining berries and warm.

Place serving of ice cream on a deep plate or shallow bowl. Cover each with ¼ of the berry mixture.

COOKING SECRET: Frozen berries may be used in the off-season and for the blended sauce.

Serves 4
Preparation Time:
  10 Minutes

Per Serving:
  290 calories,
  4 g protein,
  49 g carbohydrates,
  3 g fat

4 large scoops of vanilla low-fat ice cream or frozen yogurt
2 baskets raspberries
4 oz. Triple Sec or other orange liquer
½ small basket strawberries, cleaned, stemmed, quartered
½ basket blueberries
½ basket blackberries

Bill Cooper
Bella Saratoga
Saratoga, California

☆

Conversion Index

LIQUID MEASURES

1 dash	3 to 6 drops
1 teaspoon (tsp.)	⅓ tablespoon
1 tablespoon (Tbsp.)	3 teaspoons
1 tablespoon	½ fluid ounce
1 fluid ounce	2 tablespoons
1 cup	½ pint
1 cup	16 tablespoons
1 cup	8 fluid ounces
1 pint	2 cups
1 pint	16 fluid ounces

DRY MEASURES

1 pinch	less than ⅛ teaspoon
1 teaspoon	⅓ tablespoon
1 tablespoon	3 teaspoons
¼ cup	4 tablespoons
⅓ cup	5 tablespoons plus 1 teaspoon
½ cup	8 tablespoons
⅔ cup	10 tablespoons plus 2 teaspoons
¾ cup	12 tablespoons
1 cup	16 tablespoons

VEGETABLES AND FRUITS

Apple (1 medium)	1 cup chopped
Avocado (1 medium)	1 cup mashed
Broccoli (1 stalk)	2 cups florets
Cabbage (1 large)	10 cups, chopped
Carrot (1 medium)	½ cup, diced
Celery (3 stalks)	1 cup, diced
Eggplant (1 medium)	4 cups, cubed
Lemon (1 medium)	2 tablespoons juice
Onion (1 medium)	1 cup diced
Orange (1 medium)	½ cup juice
Parsley (1 bunch)	3 cups, chopped
Spinach (fresh), 12 cups, loosely packed	1 cup cooked
Tomato (1 medium)	¾ cup, diced
Zucchini (1 medium)	2 cups, diced

APPROXIMATE EQUIVALENTS

1 stick butter = ½ cup = 8 Tbsps. = 4 oz.
1 cup all-purpose flour = 5 oz.
1 cup cornmeal (polenta) = 4½ oz.
1 cup sugar = 8 oz.
1 cup powdered sugar = 4½ oz.
1 cup brown sugar = 6 oz.
1 large egg = 2 oz. = ¼ cup = 4 Tbsps.
1 egg yolk = 1 Tbsp. + 1 tsp.
1 egg white = 2 Tbsps. + 2 tsps.

Metric Conversion Chart

CONVERSIONS TO OUNCES TO GRAMS

To convert ounces to grams, multiply number of ounces by 28.35.

1 oz. . . . . . 30 g.	6 oz. . . . . 180 g.	11 oz. . . . 300 g.	16 oz. . . . 450 g.
2 oz. . . . . . 60 g.	7 oz. . . . . 200 g.	12 oz. . . . 340 g.	20 oz. . . . 570 g.
3 oz. . . . . . 85 g.	8 oz. . . . . 225 g.	13 oz. . . . 370 g.	24 oz. . . . 680 g.
4 oz. . . . . 115 g.	9 oz. . . . . 250 g.	14 oz. . . . 400 g.	28 oz. . . . 790 g.
5 oz. . . . . 140 g.	10 oz. . . . 285 g.	15 oz. . . . 425 g.	32 oz. . . . 900 g.

CONVERSIONS OF QUARTS TO LITERS

To convert quarts to liters, multiply number of quarts by 0.95.

1 qt. . . . . . . 1 L	2 ½ qt. . . . . 2½ L	5 qt. . . . . . 4¾ L	8 qt. . . . . . 7½ L
1½ qt. . . . . 1½ L	3 qt. . . . . . 2¾ L	6 qt. . . . . . 5½ L	9 qt. . . . . . 8½ L
2 qt. . . . . . . 2 L	4 qt. . . . . . 3¾ L	7 qt. . . . . . 6½ L	10 qt. . . . . 9½ L

CONVERSION OF FAHRENHEIT TO CELSIUS

To convert **Fahrenheit to Celsius**, subtract 32 from the Fahrenheit figure,
multiply by 5, then divide by 9.

OTHER CONVERSIONS

To convert **ounces to milliliters**, multiply number of ounces by 30.
To convert **cups to liters**, multiply number of cups by 0.24.
To convert **inches to centimeters**, multiply number of inches by 2.54.

Glossary of Ingredients

ACHIOTE: a spice blend made from ground annatto seeds, garlic, cumin, vinegar and other spices.

ACORN SQUASH: a oval-shaped winter squash with a ribbed, dark-green skin and orange flesh.

ANAHEIM CHILE: elongated and cone-shaped chiles that are red or green with a mild flavor.

ANCHO CHILE: a shiny-skinned red or green cone-shaped chile with medium heat.

ARBORIO RICE: a large-grained plump rice which equires more cooking time than other rice varieties. Arborio is traditionally used for risotto because its increased starchs lend this classic dish its creamy texture.

ARMENIAN CUCUMBER: a long, pale, green-ridged cucumber with an edible skin, also known as the English cucumber.

ARUGULA: also known as rocket or roquette, noted for its strong peppery taste. Arugula makes a lively addition to salads, soups and sautéed vegetable dishes. It's a rich source of iron as well as vitamins A and C.

ASIAN NOODLES: though some Asian-style noodles are wheat-based, many others are made from ingredients such as potato flour, rice flour, buckwheat flour and yam or soybean starch.

BALSAMIC VINEGAR: made from the juice of Trebbiano grapes and traditionally aged in barrels, this tart, sweet, rich vinegar is a versatile ingredient.

BARTLETT PEAR: this large, sweet, bell-shaped fruit has a smooth, yellow-green skin that is sometimes blushed with red.

BASMATI RICE: translated as "queen of fragrance," basmati is a long-grained rice with a nutlike flavor and fine texture.

BÉCHAMEL SAUCE: a basic French white sauce made by stirring milk into a butter-flour roux. Béchamel, the base of many other sauces, was named after its inventor, Louis XIV's steward Louis de Béchamel.

BELGIAN ENDIVE: a white, yellow-edged bitter lettuce that is crunchy.

BLOOD ORANGE: a sweet-tart, thin-skinned orange with a bright red flesh.

BOK CHOY: resembles Swiss chard with its long, thick-stemmed, light green stalks. The flavor is much like cabbage.

BOUQUET GARNI: a group of herbs, such as parsley, thyme and bay leaf, that are placed in a cheesecloth bag and tied together for the use of flavor in soups, stews and broths.

BULGUR WHEAT: wheat kernels that have been steamed, dried and crushed, offering a chewy texture.

CAPERS: available in the gourmet food sections of supermarkets, capers are a small, green, pickled bud of a Mediterranean flowering plant; usually packed in brine.

CARDAMOM: a sweetly pungent, aromatic cooking spice that is a member of the ginger family.

CHANTERELLE MUSHROOM: a trumpet-shaped mushroom that resembles an umbrella turned inside out. One of the more delicious wild mushrooms.

CHÈVRE: cheese made from goat's milk is lower in fat and offers a delicate, light and slightly earthy flavor.

CHICKPEAS: also called garbanzo beans, they have a firm texture and mild, nut-like flavor. Available canned, dried or fresh.

CHICORY or **CURLY ENDIVE:** a crisp, curly, green-leafed lettuce. Best when young. Tend to bitter with age.

CHILE OIL: a red oil available in Asian stores. Chile oil is also easily made at home by heating 1 cup of vegetable or peanut oil with 2 dozen small dried red chiles or 1 Tbsp. cayenne.

CHIPOTLE PEPPERS: ripened and smoky-flavored jalapeño peppers have a fiery heat and delicious flavor.

CHOW-CHOW: a mustard-flavored mixed vegetable and pickle relish.

CLARIFIED BUTTER: also called drawn butter. This is an unsalted butter that has been slowly melted, thereby evaporating most of the water and separating the milk solids, which sink to the bottom of the pan. After any foam is skimmed off the top, the clear butter is poured off the milk residue and used in cooking.

COCONUT MILK: available in Asian markets, this milk is noted for its richly flavored, slightly sweet taste. Coconut milk can be made by placing 2 cups of finely grated chopped fresh coconut in 3 cups scalded milk. Stir and let stand until the milk cools to room temperature. Strain before using.

COULIS: a general term referring to a thick purée or sauce.

COURT BOUILLON: a broth made by cooking various vegetables and herbs in water.

CRÈME FRAÎCHE: a bit richer than sour cream, yet more tart than whipped heavy cream. It can be purchased in most supermarkets or made by whisking together ½ cup heavy or whipping cream, not ultra-pasteurized, with ½ cup sour cream. Pour the mixture into a jar, cover and let stand in a warm, dark area for 24 hours. This will yield 1 cup which can be kept in the refrigerator for about 10 days.

CRESS: resembles radish leaves, with a hot peppery flavor.

EGGPLANT: commonly thought of as a vegetable, eggplant is actually a fruit. The very narrow, straight Japanese or Oriental eggplant has a tender, slightly sweet flesh. The Italian or baby eggplant looks like a miniature version of the common large variety, but has a more delicate skin and flesh. The egg-shaped white eggplant makes the name of this fruit understandable.

FAVA BEANS: tan flat beans that resemble very large lima beans. Fava beans can be purchased dried, canned or fresh.

FLOWERS, EDIBLE: can be stored tightly wrapped in the refrigerator, up to a week. Some of the more popular edible flowers are the peppery-flavored nasturtiums, and chive blossoms, which taste like a mild, sweet onion. Pansies and violas offer a flavor of grapes. Some of the larger flowers such as squash blossoms can be stuffed and deep-fried.

FRISÉE: sweetest of the chicory family, with a mildly bitter taste. The leaves are a pale green, slender but curly.

FROMAGE BLANC CHEESE: fresh, day-old curds with some of the whey whipped back into the cheese. The texture is similar to ricotta cheese and is available plain or flavored.

GADO-GADO: this Indonesian favorite consists of a mixture of raw and slightly cooked vegetables served with a spicy peanut sauce.

GANACHE: a rich chocolate icing made of semisweet chocolate and whipping cream that are heated and stirred together until the chocolate has melted.

GNOCCHI: the Italian word for "dumplings," gnocchi are shaped into little balls, cooked in boiling water and served with butter and Parmesan or a savory sauce. The dough can also be chilled, sliced and either baked or fried.

GORGONZOLA CHEESE: a blue-veined Italian creamy cheese.

GRAHAM FLOUR: whole-wheat flour that is slightly coarser than the regular grind.

GRITS: coarsely ground grain such as corn, oats or rice. Grits can be cooked with water or milk by boiling or baking.

HABANERO CHILE: tiny, fat, neon orange-colored chiles that are hotter than the jalapeño chile.

HAZELNUT OIL: a lightly textured oil with a rich essence of hazelnut.

HUMMUS: this thick Middle Eastern sauce is made from mashed chickpeas seasoned with lemon juice, garlic and olive oil or sesame oil.

JALAPEÑO CHILE: these plump, thumb-size green chiles are known for wonderful flavor.

JICAMA: grows underground like a tuber, yet is part of the legume family. Beneath the thick brown skin, the flesh is creamy-white and sweet. Tastes like a cross between an apple and a potato.

KALAMATA OLIVES: intensely flavored, almond-shaped, dark purple Greek olives packed in brine.

KOSHER SALT: an additive-free, coarse-grained salt that is milder than sea salt.

LEMON GRASS: available in Asian food stores, this citrus-flavored herb has long, thin, gray-green leaves and a scallion-like base. Available fresh or dried.

LENTILS: the French or European lentil is grayish-brown with a creamy flavor. The reddish-orange Egyptian or red lentil is smaller and rounder. Lentils should be stored airtight at room temperature and will keep about 6 months. Lentils offer calcium and vitamins A and B, and are a good source of iron and phosphorus.

MÂCHE: also known as lamb's lettuce, has a delicate, sweet-nutty taste. The lettuce is a deep green.

MANGO: grows in a wide variety of shapes: oblong, kidney and round. Its thin, tough skin is green and, as the fruit ripens, becomes yellow with red mottling. Under-ripe fruit can be placed in a paper bag at room temperature.

MARJORAM: there are many species of this ancient herb, which is a member of the mint family. The most widely available is sweet marjoram or wild marjoram. Early Greeks wove marjoram into funeral wreaths and planted it on graves to symbolize their loved one's happiness, both in life and beyond.

MARSALA: a wine with a rich, smoky flavor that can range from sweet to dry.

MESCLUN: a traditional French mixture of tiny lettuces, including curly endive, red lettuce, Romaine, oak-leaf, butter lettuce and rocket.

MIRIN: a sweet cooking sake.

MISO: a fermented salty soybean paste made by crushing boiled soybeans with barley.

MOREL MUSHROOM: a wild mushroom that is cone-shaped with a spongy beige cap. Has a nutty taste.

NAPA CABBAGE: also known as Chinese cabbage, it looks like a cross between celery and lettuce, very much like romaine lettuce. The flavor is more delicate with a slight peppery taste.

NASTURTIUM FLOWERS: edible sweet and peppery flowers in a rainbow of colors. Nasturtiums are beautiful in salads and easy to grow.

NORI: paper-thin sheets of dried seaweed ranging in color from dark green to dark purple to black. Nori is rich in protein, vitamins, calcium, iron and other minerals.

OPAL BASIL: a beautiful purple basil with a pungent flavor.

OREGANO: this herb belongs to the mint family and is related to both marjoram and thyme, offering a strong, pungent flavor. Greek for "joy of the mountain," oregano was almost unheard of in the U.S. until soldiers came back from Italian World War II assignments raving about it.

OYSTER MUSHROOM: a beige fan-shaped wild mushroom with a mild flavor and soft texture.

PARMESAN CHEESE: a hard dry cheese made from skimmed or partially-skimmed cow's milk.

PECORINO CHEESE: a cheese made from sheep's milk

POLENTA: cornmeal—ground corn kernels, white or yellow, often enriched with butter and grated cheese. A staple of northern Italian cooking.

PORCINI MUSHROOM: The parasol-shaped mushroom cap has a thick stem, with a meaty, smoky flavor.

QUINOA: served like rice or as a base for salads. Pale yellow in color and slightly larger than a mustard seed with a sweet flavor and soft texture.

RADICCHIO: this peppery-tasting lettuce with brilliant, ruby-colored leaves is available year-round, with a peak season from mid-winter to early spring. Choose heads that have crisp, full-colored leaves with no sign of browning. Store in a plastic bag in the refrigerator for up to a week.

RICE WINE VINEGAR: a light, clean-tasting vinegar that works perfectly as is, in salads, as well as in a variety of Asian-inspired dishes.

RISOTTO: an Italian rice specialty made by stirring hot stock in Arborio rice that has been sautéed in butter.

ROMAINE: known for a sweet nutty flavor, this lettuce has long, crisp, green or red leaves.

ROUX: a mixture of melted butter or oil and flour used to thicken sauces, soups and stews. Sprinkle flour into the melted, bubbling-hot butter, whisking constantly over low heat, cooking at least 2 minutes.

SAFFRON: a bright yellow, strongly aromatic spice that imparts a unique flavor. Store saffron in a cool dark place for up to 6 months.

SAVOY CABBAGE: also known as curly cabbage, has lacy leaves with a white or reddish trim.

SERRANO CHILE: a fat, squat, red or green hot chile. They are milder when roasted with the ribs and seeds removed.

SHIITAKE MUSHROOM: a Japanese mushroom sold fresh or dried, which imparts a distinctively rich flavor to any dish. The versatile shiitake is suitable for almost any cooking method including sautéing, broiling and baking.

SNOW PEAS: a translucent, bright green pod that is thin, crisp and entirely edible. The tiny seeds inside are tender and sweet. Snow peas are also called Chinese snow peas and sugar peas.

SORBET: a palate refresher between courses or as a dessert, the sorbet never contains milk and often has softer consistency than sherbet.

SOY MILK: higher in protein than cow's milk, this milky, iron-rich liquid is a non-dairy product made by pressing ground, cooked soybeans. Cholesterol-free and low in calcium, fat and sodium, it makes an excellent milk substitute.

SPAGHETTI SQUASH: a yellow watermelon-shaped squash whose flesh, when cooked, separates into spaghetti-like strands.

STRUDEL: a type of pastry made up of many layers of very thin dough spread with a filling, then rolled and baked until crisp.

SUN-DRIED TOMATOES: air-dried tomatoes sold in various forms such as marinated tomato halves, which are packed in olive oil, or a tapenade, which is puréed dried tomatoes in olive oil with garlic.

TAHINI: Middle Eastern in origin, tahini is made from crushed sesame seeds. Used mainly for its creamy, rich and nutty flavor as well as for binding food together.

TEMPEH: made from cultured, fermented soybeans; comes in flat, light, grainy-looking cakes.

TOFU: a versatile fresh soybean curd, tofu is an excellent and inexpensive form of protein. It is characteristically bland in taste, but can be enhanced with seasonings.

TOMATILLOS: green husk tomatoes; small with a tart, citrus-like flavor .

TRUFFLE: a fungus that grows underground near the roots of trees prized by gourmets for centuries. Truffles should be used as soon as possible after purchase, but can be stored up to 6 days in the refrigerator or for several months in the freezer. Canned truffles, truffle paste and frozen truffles can be found in specialty stores.

VIDALIA ONION: the namesake of Vidalia, Georgia where they thrive. This yellow onion, sweet and juicy, is available in the summer or by mail- order year-round.

WATERCRESS: this spicy-flavored green is dark in color with glossy leaves.

Mail Order Sources

If you are unable to locate some of the specialty food products used in *Cooking Secrets for Healthy Living*, you can order them from the mail order sources listed below. These items are delivered by UPS, fully insured and at reasonable shipping costs.

COFFEE AND TEA ALTERNATIVES

Adamba Imports
585 Meserole Street
Brooklyn, NY 11237
718-628-9700
For Inka

Celestial Seasonings
4600 Sleepytime Drive
Boulder, CO 80301
303-530-5300
Large assortment of herbal teas.

Worthington Foods
900 Proprietors Road
Worthington, OH 43085
614-885-9511
For Kaffree Roma

COFFEE AND TEA

Brown & Jenkins Trading Co.
P.O. Box 2306
South Burlington,
VT 05407-2306
(802)862-2395
(800) 456-JAVA
Water-decaffeinated coffees featuring over 30 blends such as Brown

& Jenkins Special blend, Vermont Breakfast blend and Hawaiian Kona, in addition to 15 different flavors of teas.

Stash Tea Co.
P.O. Box 90
Portland, OR 97207
(503) 684-7944
(800) 826-4218
Earl Grey, herbal teas like peppermint, ruby mint, orange spice and licorice flavors.

DRIED BEANS AND PEAS

Baer's Best
154 Green Street
Reading, MA 01867
(617) 944-8719
Bulk or 1-pound packages of over 30 different varieties of beans, common to exotic. No peas.

The Bean Bag
818 Jefferson Street
Oakland, CA 94607
510-839-8988
Dried beans, including many heirloom and organic beans, and bean mixes; hot sauces; sun-dried tomatoes; gourmet rices, specialty grains.

Corti Brothers
5801 Folsom Blvd.
Sacramento, CA 95819
(916) 736-3800
Special gourmet items such as: imported extra-virgin olive oils, wines, exotic beans, egg pasta.

Dean & Deluca
560 Broadway
New York, NY 10012
(800) 221-7714
(212) 431-1691
Dried beans, salted capers, polenta, arborio rice, dried mushrooms, dried tomatoes, parmesan and reggiano cheeses, kitchen and baking equipment.

Phipps Ranch
P.O. Box 349
Pescadero, CA 94060
415-879-0787
Dried beans such as cannellini, cranberry, fava, flageolet, borlotti, scarlet runner, Tongues of Fire, and more. Also dried peas, herb vinegars, grains, herbs and spices.

DRIED MUSHROOMS

Dean & Deluca
560 Broadway
New York, NY 10012
(800) 221-7714
(212) 431-1691
*Dried beans, salted capers,
polenta, arborio rice, dried mushrooms, dried tomatoes, parmesan
and reggiano cheeses, kitchen and
baking equipment.*

G.B. Ratto & Co.
821 Washington St.
Oakland, CA 94607
(800) 325-3483
(510) 836-2250 fax
*Imported pasta, dried beans,
amaretti cookies, semolina flour,
dried mushrooms, dried tomatoes,
parmesan and reggiano cheeses.*

Gold Mine Natural Food Co.
1947 30th St.
San Diego, CA 92102-1105
(800) 475-3663
*Organic foods, dried foods, whole
grain rice, Asian dried mushrooms, condiments, sweeteners,
spices.*

FLOURS AND GRAINS

Arrowhead Mills
Box 2059
Hereford, TX 79045
806-364-0730
*A large variety of whole grain prod-
ucts, including specialty grains, grain
mixes, flours, cereals.*

Barbara's Bakery, Inc.
3900 Cypress Drive
Petaluma, CA 94954
707-765-2263
Whole grain and cereal products.

Butte Creek Mill
P.O. Box 561
Eagle Point, Oregon 97524
503-826-3531
*A large assortment of cereals,
whole grains, rolled grains, stone-
ground flours and meals.*

Continental Mills
P.O. Box 88176
Seattle, WA 98138
206-872-8400
*Specialty whole grains, including
bulgur.*

Dean & Deluca
560 Broadway
New York, NY 10012
(800) 221-7714
(212) 431-1691
*Dried beans, salted capers,
polenta, arborio rice, dried mushrooms, dried tomatoes, parmesan
and reggiano cheeses, kitchen and
baking equipment.*

G.B. Ratto & Co.
821 Washington Street
Oakland, CA 94607
(510) 832-6503
(800) 325-3483
*Flours, rice, bulgar wheat, couscous,
oils, and sun-dried tomatoes.*

Gold Mine Natural Food Co.
1947 30th St.
San Diego, CA 92102-1105
(800) 475-3663
*Organic foods, dried foods, whole
grain rice, Asian dried mushrooms, condiments, sweeteners,
spices.*

King Arthur Flour Baker's Catalogue
P.O. Box 876
Norwich, VT 05055
(800) 827-6836
*Semolina flour, all types of flours,
wheat berries, kitchen and baking
equipment.*

Lundberg Family Farms
P.O. Box 369
Richvale, CA 95974-0369
916-882-4551
*Premium short-grain and long-
grain brown rice. California basmati brown rice, organic brown
rice, specialty brown rices and rice
blends, rice cakes and rice cereals.*

Specialty Rice Marketing Inc.
P.O. Box 880
Brinkley, AR 72021
501-734-1234
Whole grains and cereals, including brown rice cereal.

U.S. Mills
4301 N. 30th Street
Omaha, NE 6811
402-451-4567
Whole grains and cereals, including brown rice cereals.

The Vermont Country Store
P.O. Box 3000
Manchester Center,
VT 05255-3000
(802) 362-2400
credit card orders
(802) 362-4647
customer service
Orders are taken 24 hours a day. Many different varieties: whole wheat, sweet-cracked, stone-ground rye, buckwheat, cornmeal and many more. They also sell a variety of items which are made in Vermont.

FRUIT & VEGETABLES

Diamond Organics
Freedom, CA 95019
(800) 922-2396
Free catalog available. Fresh, organically grown fruits & vegetables, specialty greens, roots, sprouts, exotic fruits, citrus, wheat grass.

Giant Artichoke
11241 Merritt St.
Castroville, CA 95012
(408) 633-2778
Fresh baby artichokes.

Lee Anderson's Covalda Date Company
51-392 Harrison Street
(Old Highway 86)
P.O. Box 908
Coachella, CA 92236-0908
(619) 398-3441
Organic dates, raw date sugar and other date products. Also dried fruits, nuts and seeds.

Northwest Select
14724 184th St. NE
Arlington, WA 98223
(800) 852-7132
(206) 435-8577
Fresh baby artichokes.

Timber Crest Farms
4791 Dry Creek Road
Healdsburg, CA 95448
(707) 433-8251
Domestic dried tomatoes and other unsulfured dried fruits and nuts.

HONEY

Howard's Happy Honeybees
4828 Morro Drive
Bakersfield, CA 93307
(805) 366-4962
Unfiltered flavored honeys, such as orange blossom and sage honeys in addition to honey candy.

KITCHEN AND BAKING EQUIPMENT

A Cook's Wares
211 37th St.
Beaver Falls, PA 15010-2103
(412) 846-9490

All-Clad Metalcrafters
RD#2
Canonsburg, PA 15317
412-745-8300
Premium nonstick cookware.

Dean & Deluca

560 Broadway
New York, NY 10012
(800) 221-7714
(212) 431-1691
Dried beans, salted capers, polenta, arborio rice, dried mushrooms, dried tomatoes, parmesan and reggiano cheeses, kitchen and baking equipment.

La Cuisine

323 Cameron St.
Alexandria, VA 22314
(800)521-1176

The Chef's Catalog

3215 Commercial Ave.
Northbrook, IL 60062-1900
(800) 338-3232
(708) 480-8929

Williams-Sonoma

Mail Order Dept.
P.O. Box 7456
San Francisco,
CA 94120-7456
(800) 541-2233
credit card orders
(800) 541-1262
customer service
Vinegars, oils, foods and kitchenware.

MEAT SUBSTITUTES

Boca Burger

1660 N.E. 12th Terrace
Fort Lauderdale, FL 33305
305-524-1977
Textured soy protein product line.

Harvest Direct

P.O. Box 4514
Decatur, IL 62525
800-8-FLAVOR
Fat-free texturized vegetable protein.

Knox Mountain Foods

5 Knox Mountain Rd.
Sandbornton, NH 03256
603-934-6960
Seitan mixes and sausages.

Yves Fine Foods

1138 E. Georgia Street
Vancouver, BC,
Canada V6A 2A8
604-251-1345
Veggie wieners and deli slices.

PASTA & SAUCES

ConAgra

Five ConAgra Drive
Omaha, NE 68102-5006
800-328-3738
Fat-free pasta sauces, soups and beans.

Corti Brothers

5801 Folsom Blvd.
Sacramento, CA 95819
(916) 736-3800
Special gourmet items such as: imported extra-virgin olive oils, exotic beans, egg pasta.

G.B. Ratto & Co.

821 Washington St.
Oakland, CA 94607
(800) 325-3483
(510) 836-2250 fax
Imported pasta, dried beans, semolina flour, dried mushrooms, dried tomatoes.

Organic Food Products

P.O. Box 1510
Freedom, CA 95019
408-685-6575
Fat-free pasta sauces.

Morisi's Pasta

John Morisi & Sons, Inc.
647 Fifth Avenue
Brooklyn, NY 11215
(718) 499-0146
(800) 253-6044
Over 250 varieties available from this 50-year old, family-owned gourmet pasta business.

SAFFRON

Vanilla Saffron Imports, Inc.
949 Valencia Street
San Francisco, CA 94110
(415) 648-8990
(415) 648-2240 fax
Saffron, vanilla beans and pure vanilla extract, dried mushrooms as well as herbs.

SEEDS FOR GROWING HERBS AND VEGETABLES

Herb Gathering, Inc.
5742 Kenwood Ave.
Kansas City, MO 64110
(816) 523-2653
Seeds for growing herbs, fresh-cut herbs.

Shepherd's Garden Seeds
6116 Highway 9
Felton, CA 95018
(408) 335-6910
Excellent selection of vegetable and herb seeds with growing instructions.

The Cook's Garden
P.O. Box 535
Londonderry, VT 05148
(802) 824-3400
Organically grown, reasonably priced vegetable, herb and flower seeds. Illustrated catalog has growing tips and recipes.

Vermont Bean Seed Company
Garden Lane
Fair Haven VT 05743
(802) 273-3400
Selling over 60 different varieties of beans, peas, corn, tomato and flower seeds.

W. Atlee Burpee & Co.
Warminster, PA 18974
(800) 888-1447
Well-known, reliable, full-color seed catalog.

Well-Sweep Herb Farm
317 Mount Bethal Rd.
Port Murray, NJ 07865
(908) 852-5390
Seeds for growing herbs, fresh herb plants.

SPECIALTY FOODS AND FOOD GIFTS

China Moon Catalogue
639 Post St.
San Francisco, CA 94109
(415) 771-MOON (6666)
(415) 775-1409 fax
Chinese oils, peppers, teas, salts, beans, candied ginger, kitchen supplies, cookbooks.

Corti Brothers
5801 Folsom Blvd.
Sacramento, CA 95819
(916) 736-3800
Special gourmet items such as: imported extra-virgin olive oils, wines, exotic beans, egg pasta.

Festive Foods
9420 Arroyo Lane
Colorado Springs, CO 80908
(719) 495-2339
Spices and herbs, teas, oils, vinegars, chocolate and baking ingredients.

G.B. Ratto & Co.
821 Washington St.
Oakland, CA 94607
(800) 325-3483
(510) 836-2250 fax
Imported pasta, dried beans, amaretti cookies, semolina flour, dried mushrooms, dried tomatoes, parmesan and reggiano cheeses.

Gazin's Inc.
P.O. Box 19221
New Orleans, LA 70179
(504) 482-0302
Specializing in Cajun, Creole and New Orleans foods.

Gold Mine Natural Food Co.
1947 30th St.
San Diego, CA 92102-1105
(800) 475-3663
Organic foods, dried foods, whole grain rice, Asian dried mushrooms, condiments, sweeteners, spices.

Knott's Berry Farm
8039 Beach Boulevard
Buena Park, CA 90620
(800) 877-6887
(714) 827-1776
*Eleven types of jams and
preserves, nine of which are
non-sugar.*

Kozlowski Farms
5566 Gravenstein Highway
Forestville, CA 95436
(707) 887-1587
(800) 473-2767
*Jams, jellies, barbecue and steak
sauces, conserves, honeys, salsas,
chutneys and mustards. Some
products are non-sugared, others
are in the organic line. You can
customize your order from 65
different products.*

Williams-Sonoma
Mail Order Dept.
P.O. Box 7456
San Francisco,
CA 94120-7456
(800) 541-2233
credit card orders
(800) 541-1262
customer service
*Vinegars, oils, foods and
kitchenware.*

SPICES AND HERBS

**Apple Pie Farm, Inc.
(The Herb Patch)**
Union Hill Rd. #5
Malvern, PA 19355
(215)933-4215
A wide variety of fresh-cut herbs.

Festive Foods
9420 Arroyo Lane
Colorado Springs, CO 80908
(719) 495-2339
*Spices and herbs, teas, oils, vinegars,
chocolate and baking ingredients.*

Fox Hill Farm
444 West Michigan Avenue
P.O.Box 9
Parma, MI 49269
(517) 531-3179
*Fresh-cut herb plants, topiaries,
ornamental and medicinal herbs.*

**Meadowbrook Herb
Gardens**
Route 138
Wyoming, RI 02898
(401) 539-7603
*Organically grown herb season-
ings, high quality spice and teas.*

Nichols Garden Nursery
1190 N. Pacific Hwy
Albany, OR 97321
(503) 928-9280
Fresh herb plants.

**Old Southwest Trading
Company**
P.O.Box 7545
Albuquerque, NM 87194
(800) 748-2861
(505) 831-5144
*Specializes in chiles, everything
from dried chiles to canned chiles
and other chile-related products.*

**Penzey Spice House
Limited**
P.O. Box 1633
Milwaukee, WI 53201
(414) 768-8799
*Fresh ground spices (saffron, cin-
namon and peppers), bulk spices,
seeds, and seasoning mixes.*

Rafal Spice Company
2521 Russell Street
Detroit, MI 48207
(800) 228-4276
(313) 259-6373
*Seasoning mixtures, herbs, spices,
oil, coffee beans and teas.*

Spice Merchant
P.O. Box 524
Jackson Hole, WY 83001
(307) 733-7811
Specializes in Asian spices.

VERMONT MAPLE SYRUP

Butternut Mountain Farm
P.O.Box 381
Johnson, VT 05656
(802) 635-7483
(800) 828-2376
*Different grades of maple syrup,
also a variety of honey and fruit
syrups such as raspberry and
blueberry.*

**Green Mountain
Sugar House**
R.F.D. #1
Ludlow, VT 05149
(802) 228-7151
(800) 647-7006
*Different grades of maple syrup,
maple cream and maple candies,
in addition to cheese, fudge and
creamed honey.*

VINEGARS AND OILS

Community Kitchens
P.O. Box 2311, Dept. J-D
Baton Rouge, LA 70821-2311
(800) 535-9901
*Vinegars and oil, in addition to
meats, crawfish, coffees and teas.*

Corti Brothers
5801 Folsom Blvd.
Sacramento, CA 95819
(916) 736-3800
*Special gourmet items such as:
imported extra-virgin olive oils,
wines, exotic beans, egg pasta.*

Festive Foods
9420 Arroyo Lane
Colorado Springs, CO 80908
(719) 495-2339
*Spices and herbs, teas, oils,
vinegars, chocolate and baking
ingredients.*

**Kermit Lynch Wine
Merchant**
1605 San Pablo Ave.
Berkeley, CA 94702-1317
(510) 524-1524
(510) 528-7026 fax

**Kimberly Wine
Vinegar Works**
290 Pierce Street
Daly City, CA 94015
(415) 755-0306
*Fine wine vinegars and northern
California olive oil.*

Select Origins
Box N
Southampton, NY 11968
(516) 288-1382
(800) 822-2092
Oils, vinegars and rice.

Williams-Sonoma
Mail Order Dept.
P.O. Box 7456
San Francisco,
CA 94120-7456
(800) 541-2233
credit card orders
(800) 541-1262
customer service
*Vinegars, oils, foods and
kitchenware.*

Herb Sources

Newsletters and classes are available through the following gardens.

Brooklyn Botanic Garden
Education Department
1000 Washington Avenue
Brooklyn, NY 11225-1099
(718) 941-4044

Caprilands Herb Farm
Darlene Lee
534 Silver St.
Coventry, CT 06238
(203) 742-7244

Cats in the Cradle
Christine Whitmann
Rt. 140
Alton, NH 03809

Cecily Gill Herb Garden
Tucson Botanical Gardens
2150 N. Alvernon Way
Tucson, AZ 85712
(602) 326-9686

England's Herb Farm
Yvonne England
RD 1, Box 706
Honey Brook, PA 19344
(215) 273-2863

Farmington Historic Home and Garden
3033 Bardstown Rd.
Louisville, KY 40205
(502) 452-9920

Hancock Shaker Village
P.O. Box 898
Rte. 20
Pittsfield, MA 01202

Heard's Country Gardens
Mary Lou Heard
14391 Edwards St.
Westminster, CA 92683
(714) 894-2444

The Herbs of Happy Hill
Kathy Chain
14705 Happy Hill Rd.
Chester, VA 23831
(804) 796-2762

Houston Garden Center
1500 Hermann Dr.
Houston, TX 77004
(713) 529-5371

Iowa State University Horticultural Garden
Ames, IA 50011
(515) 294-2751

Kingwood Center
Bill Collins
900 Park Ave. West
Mansfield, OH 44906
(419) 522-0211

Longwood Gardens
P.O. Box 501
Kennett Square,
PA 19348-0501
(215) 388-6741

Michigan 4-H Children's Garden
4700 S. Hagadorn Rd.
East Lansing, MI 48823
(517) 353-6692

New Hampshire Farm Museum
Susie McKinley and
Melissa Walker
Rt. 125, Plummer's Ridge
P.O. Box 644
Milton, NH 03851
(603) 652-7840

Oak Valley Herb Farm
Kathy Keville
14648 Pear Tree Lane
Nevada City, CA 95959

Pettengill Farm
Jan Richenburg
121 Ferry Rd.
Salisbury, MA 01952
(508) 462-3675

Quail Botanical Gardens
P.O. 230005
Encinitas, CA 92023-0005
(619) 436-3036

San Antonio Botanical Gardens
Paul Cox
555 Funston Place
San Antonio, TX 78209
(210) 821-5143

The Shaker Messenger
Diana Van Kolken
210 South River Ave.
Holland, MI 49423
(616) 396-4588

Silver Bay Herb Farm
Mary Preus
9151 Tracyton Blvd.
Bremerton, WA 98310
(206) 692-1340

**State Arboretum
of Virginia**
Friends of the State
Arboretum
P.O. Box 175
Boyce, VA 22620
(703) 837-1458

**Thomas Jefferson Center
for Historic Plants**
John T. Fitzpatrick
Monticello
P.O. Box 316
Charlottesville, VA 22902
(804) 979-5283

**United Society of
Shakers—Workshops**
R.R. 1, Box 640
Poland Spring, ME 04274
(207) 926-4597

**University of California
Botanical Garden**
Centennial Dr.
Berkeley CA 94720

Here's a listing of newsletters
and other herbal publications:

**The American Herb
Association Quarterly
Newsletter**
Kathi Keville, Editor
P.O. Box 1673
Nevada City, CA 95959
*(This newsletter is included with
membership in the American
Herb Association)*

Country Thyme Gazette
Theresa Loe
P.O. Box 3090
El Segundo, CA 90245
(310) 322-6026

**Foster's Botanical and
Herb Reviews**
Steven Foster
P.O. Box 106
Eureka Springs, AR 72632
(501) 253-7309

Recipe Index

About the Author

KATHLEEN DEVANNA FISH, author of the popular "Secrets" series, is a gourmet cook and gardener who is always on the lookout for recipes with style and character.

In addition to *Cooking Secrets for Healthy Living,* the California native has written the award-winning *Great Vegetarian Cookbook, The Gardener's Cookbook, The Great California Cookbook, California Wine Country Cooking Secrets, San Francisco's Cooking Secrets, Monterey's Cooking Secrets, New England's Cooking Secrets, Cape Cod's Cooking Secrets, Pacific Northwest Cooking Secrets* and *Cooking and Traveling Inn Style.*

Before embarking on a writing and publishing career, she owned and operated three businesses in the travel and hospitality industry.

ROBERT FISH, award-winning photojournalist, produces the images that bring together the concept of the "Secrets" series.

In addition to taking the cover photographs, Robert explores the food and wine of each region, helping to develop the overview upon which each book is based.

Bon Vivant Press

A division of The Millennium Publishing Group
P.O. Box 1994
Monterey, CA 93942
800-524-6826
408-373-0592
408-373-3567 FAX

Send _____ copies of *Cooking Secrets for Healthy Living* at $15.95 each.

Send _____ copies of *Pacific Northwest Cooking Secrets* at $15.95 each.

Send _____ copies of *The Great California Cookbook* at $14.95 each.

Send _____ copies of *The Gardener's Cookbook* at $15.95 each.

Send _____ copies of *The Great Vegetarian Cookbook* at $15.95 each.

Send _____ copies of *California Wine Country Cooking Secrets* at $14.95 each.

Send _____ copies of *San Francisco's Cooking Secrets* at $13.95 each.

Send _____ copies of *Monterey's Cooking Secrets* at $13.95 each.

Send _____ copies of *New England's Cooking Secrets* at $14.95 each.

Send _____ copies of *Cape Cod's Cooking Secrets* at $14.95 each.

Add $3.00 postage and handling for the first book ordered and $1.50 for each additional book. Please add $1.08 sales tax per book, for those books shipped to California addresses.

Please charge my ☐ Visa
☐ MasterCard # _____

Expiration date _____ Signature _____

Enclosed is my check for _____

Name _____

Address _____

City _____ State _____ Zip _____

☐ This is a gift. Send directly to:

Name _____

Address _____

City _____ State _____ Zip _____

☐ Autographed by the author
  Autographed to _____

NOTES